Once again for Ngo Duc Thang,
best and most patient pal ever

DESTINATION

CAMBODIA

ADVENTURES
IN THE KINGDOM

WALTER MASON

ALLEN&UNWIN
SYDNEY · MELBOURNE · AUCKLAND · LONDON

First published in 2013

Allen & Unwin
83 Alexander Street
Crows Nest NSW 2065
Australia
Phone: (61 2) 8425 0100
Email: info@allenandunwin.com
Web: www.allenandunwin.com

Cataloguing-in-Publication details are available
from the National Library of Australia
www.trove.nla.gov.au

ISBN 978 1 74237 662 2

Set in 12/15.5 pt Adobe Garamond by Post Pre-press Group, Australia
Printed in Australia by McPherson's Printing Group

10 9 8 7 6 5 4 3 2 1

DESTINATION
CAMBODIA

CONTENTS

WALTER MASON

ACKNOWLEDGEMENTS

Every day I learn more about the beauty and goodness of my lifelong companion, Ngo Duc Thang, and every day he surprises me—this book is as much his creation as mine.

I bless and thank my publishers: Maggie Hamilton, recently retired, and Sue Hines, constantly patient. All the people who make up the team at Allen & Unwin represent some of the smartest, most devoted and impeccably bookish people on earth, and I am so proud to be associated with them.

The dear friends and inspirations in Cambodia who have been so generous with their time, their affection and their wisdom: Suong Mak and Tola, Chhai Kakkada, Sok Chanphal, Lang Kosal, Heng Kimly, Hang Borin and his family, Sok Huy and all the others. Thank you for being interested in me and my project and for inviting me into your lives. You have all been incredible teachers. Also to my long lost friend, Pek Vannak—I hope you are well, wherever you are, and I hope we will meet again one day.

My friends in Australia who have remained loyal and excited and believe in me as a writer: Long Hoang, Angus Nalder, Tim Graham, Rosamund Burton and Stephanie Dowrick.

I was once a bookseller and will always be one in my heart. I salute all of Australia's brilliant and eccentric booksellers, but would like to single out just a few who went above and beyond in their support for me: Barbara and Tony Horgan at Shearer's, Derek Dryden, Karen Ferris, Sue Cole and Kerry McIlroy.

On occasion I needed help, contacts and information in Cambodia, and Acey Teasdale and James Gerrand provided invaluable assistance.

Finally to my beloved family, who put up with my boasting and long stories: my mum and dad, and Chantel and Daniel; the adorable little Latus, Ivy and Jonah, and Nguyen Trung Kien, who keeps me alive when I am in Asia.

INTRODUCTION

I first went to Cambodia as a young man because it seemed the most exotic and dangerous place in the world to go. Like so many others, I was drawn by its recent history of tragedy, its continued lack of stability and its tremendous ruins at Angkor Wat. I also went because my mother had specifically asked me not to, and I was still at the age where annoying my mother was something I delighted in. Now I feel ashamed of most of those reasons, especially as I quickly learned that Cambodia's was an ancient and complex culture where real people dealt with real problems and had immediate and far more pressing concerns that more or less ignored all of the romantic obsessions I had brought with me.

So I began to go back to Cambodia over the years, taking the short trip from Ho Chi Minh City to Phnom

Penh whenever I could, meeting and losing friends and watching Cambodia change. I also watched Phnom Penh grow into one of Asia's most enchanting cities, the kind of place that traps expatriates, artists and writers and renders them all fiercely protective of their adopted home.

Cambodia became a place that obsessed me. I slowly built up an enormous library of books about it, and began to count members of the Cambodian diaspora among my friends, neighbours and spiritual advisors. I taught English to Buddhist monks in a ramshackle Cambodian monastery in the suburbs of Sydney, I ate at the one or two Cambodian noodle bars nearby, and I dreamed of Phnom Penh, always.

Most of my trips to Cambodia were, of necessity, short, but they took place over a number of years, allowing me to really be aware of the enormous changes happening there. When I knew I would be writing this book I took two, much longer, trips and it was during these that I collected most of the stories you will read here.

Many of the things that enchant me about Cambodia also serve to aggravate me sometimes. The clear and sometimes prim morality of the Cambodian people occasionally infuriates me, but at the same time I appreciate the tremendous kindness they show to each other, and the depth of consideration they have for the sufferings of all. There is a consciousness that all are linked in this chain of suffering, and those without gratitude or mercy are viewed with suspicion and contempt.

People are shy, but once you have their trust they include you so completely in their lives that it can become bewildering. Cambodians have a passion for communication, and are happiest when surrounded with people. In this high-tech age people have extended that sense of communication to embrace all kinds of technology, and the frenzied connection continues via telephones and Facebook. The poverty of most everyone I know causes them to be energetic and resourceful, but hardly anyone is willing to sacrifice friendship for any kind of financial gain.

Perhaps more than any other country in the world at the moment, Cambodia is the subject of speed tourism. Vast tour groups from many countries fly in for two or three days, often only visiting the ruins of Angkor, then leave again. It is such a shame, because Phnom Penh, Cambodia's capital, is an exquisite place that offers some of the finest comforts available in Asia, and Cambodia's small towns and cities are almost universally beguiling, with their remnants of colonial architecture, their slightly scuffed appearance and their quiet and shy but smiling inhabitants. Almost any detour off the beaten track in Cambodia is immensely rewarding, though accomplishing it may not be easy.

I realise I've barely mentioned Angkor Wat in this book, but that is perhaps a reaction to the fact that, after the despicable Pol Pot period, it is the subject of most other books about Cambodia. There is no denying its hypnotic fascination. Nothing can beat that first sight of it as you approach in the early morning. No-one is prepared for its size or its majesty. I am secretly an Angkor tragic, my interest fuelled by a lesser-known Cambodian obsession with the occult meanings of Angkor Wat and its prophetic purpose.

But this book is about the people of Cambodia, my friends and acquaintances who have enriched my life with their love, their warmth and their profound generosity. I can't ignore some of the tragic elements of Cambodian history as much as I might have wanted to. The fact is that in Cambodia, the history of the Khmer Rouge years still lives, and everyone still talks about it, even people born years after its end. I have a feeling Cambodia will remain haunted by its past for several generations to come.

Yet there is so much more to Cambodia, its people and its culture than skulls, destruction and ruins. I hope I will convey to you the ever-present sense of magic that is alive in Cambodia, the wonderful ways in which people express their spiritual ideas in their everyday lives, and the great attention to small aesthetic detail. And I make no apologies for frequently alluding to the tremendous physical beauty of the Cambodian people. It is there, it is noteworthy, and I will not deny it.

Cambodia is rich in beauty. Its stark, unique rural landscape—dry for so much of the year until it floods and becomes rich and fruitful—is often invoked by its

people, who all romanticise an idea of rurality that sometimes hides the starker truths of poverty, malnutrition
and lack of access to education and health services. But
one of the most remarkable days in my life was spent in
the rice fields of Kompong Speu in the dry season. I was
in the company of a farmer who knew no English, and
we spent the day collecting the fruits of the ubiquitous
palm trees, the juice of which he would later turn into
sugar.

When we finally reached the river, muddy and brown
at this hottest and driest part of the year, we ate the
parcels of sticky rice and dried fish he had carried for us,
and then, with no words at all, we stripped and plunged
into the thick water. Nothing had ever seemed colder
or more refreshing, though when we emerged we were
covered in a viscous brown sheen that I retained till I
showered in my pristine hotel room later that night.

As we walked home we stumbled upon a line of
young monks picking their way along the narrow paths
that delineate the rice paddies. They shrieked and ran
towards us when they saw us, boys once again, forgetting their monastic vows of sobriety and self-possession.
And suddenly I was aware of the gifts of this remarkable
place—a simple, unpretentious hospitality and a willingness to allow me, a stranger, into their world if I was
willing to accept them as they were.

I carry parts of Cambodia with me always, not least
because the incredibly tech-savvy inhabitants of Phnom

Penh are constantly online, and at any time of the day or night I am likely to receive an SMS, email or Facebook message from a monk, a hairdresser, a composer or a sandwich hand asking me how things are and telling me all the latest gossip. But I have also been changed by the manners and attitudes of my Cambodian friends, and the sensibilities I picked up during my longer stays in their country. A more careful attention to the pride and dignity of others, a softer and more forgiving approach to friends' foibles, and a capacity to simply sit and wait, because it will all happen at the right time.

I hope this book will bring alive some of the charms of Cambodia, whether you have visited it before or not. The lavishly and extravagantly painted temple interiors, the presence of old spirits and ghostly guardians, and the sometimes down-at-heel, but always exquisite, symmetry of its architecture and art. This is an account of my memories and experiences. I don't seek to tell the story of Cambodian history—that has been done so much better in greater books. I don't claim to speak for Cambodians, or understand completely their culture. All I have done is tell you some of the stories of the wonderful and fascinating people I encountered during my journeys. They have blessed me with their spirit, their good humour and their stories. I hope you will love them as much as I do.

LOOKING FOR PEK VANNAK

Pek Vannak had once been my friend. But that was a long time ago in a very different Cambodia: in 1996, when I first visited, we had been inseparable companions exploring a scarred and crazy Phnom Penh that barely felt like a town at all. Now he was lost, he had been lost for years, and who knew where he was. Maybe in America? He had always said he had close family in America, and he had shown me their photographs and their letters. These were sacred objects to him. Maybe he had been one of the lucky few who had made it and was living his dream in some obscure suburb of Houston or New Jersey. But I wanted to find him, to make this connection with my fractured past, and so I enlisted one of my friends, Mak, to come with me to his old street address. Having been back in Cambodia just a few days, I found myself thinking of Pek Vannak constantly.

Walking up and down the street I was totally lost. There was nothing to remind me of those nights sixteen years ago when we would sit in his front room watching TV and eating barbecued chicken on skewers. This was the middle of the day, there was a thriving, stinking market on the street, and people were everywhere. At last arriving at the address, my heart sank. There stood before us a massive new building, maybe only two years old, one that had swallowed up a half-dozen of the old shop houses that once stood there, Pek Vannak's among them.

We began asking people if they had known him. No-one had. People were helpful, even curious, but, they explained politely, these shops were all new and all the old people had moved out long ago. There was a man on the street fixing watches at a little wooden box. He looked old and comfortable, the type of guy you can imagine had done exactly the same thing for sixteen years.

'What did you say his name was?' he asked, cocking a deaf ear to our enquiries. Mak was clutching a piece of paper on which I had written the old address, the one where I used to send letters, postcards and photographs. It was written in English, of course, but the old guy stared at it bravely for a moment.

'Can't help you,' he said, handing it back. 'I can't speak English.'

I jumped forward, insisting we keep trying. 'But tell him what Pek looked like. He was so distinctive—short and slim but horribly scarred, his nose and lips half torn away.'

The old man laughed when this description was translated to him. 'Well, that's not a face you'd be likely to forget,' he said. 'But I'm certain—no-one lives around here who looks like that.'

'How long have you been here?' we asked.

'Two years, maybe three,' he said, looking apologetic. When he noticed my sad face he looked concerned and said, 'I hope you find your friend. You are a good man to remember an old friend like that. I hope you can be reunited.'

We walked doggedly up and down the street, staring hopefully into houses and shops, asking shop assistants and soft-drink sellers and *motoduhps*, but all of them shook their heads and smiled in an embarrassed, apologetic way, hoping we'd go away and not ask them more questions. Pek Vannak's house had been bulldozed, there was no getting away from the fact. It had been replaced with a pink faux-marble edifice that housed jewellery shops on its ground floor and apartments above. My search was hopeless.

And yet it felt so good to look for him, even if I couldn't find him. I was talking about him, and people were engaged in my search, in my interest. People were treating me with sympathy and kindness, as a person who needed help. It brought out the best in everyone. Mak told me there is a TV show that reunites people lost during Pol Pot times. Maybe you could go on that, he suggested. I considered the possibility.

Memories of the friends of one's youth always remain the most powerful. The myth of Pek Vannak had grown in my mind over the years. His absence, his difference, his vulnerability—all had become exaggerated totems for me, taunting me with my own lack of constancy, my own failures as a friend: I had never sent him money and in the end I had stopped communicating with him. And now he was lost, forever.

Back in 1996 I was a much younger man, dazed and confused and wandering around Phnom Penh like the lost soul I was. I spent much of my day on the grounds of Wat Koh, at that time a busy urban monastery packed to the gills with young monks. I was enchanted by the place, and would be up at four in the morning in order to get to prayers on time and then hang out in the monks' quarters.

The monks there were all wonderful characters. The old ones were very thin and somewhat haunted, all of them survivors of the Khmer Rouge times and many of them veterans of one army or another; it pays not to ask in Cambodia. As Nic Dunlop, biographer of Comrade Duch, one of the Khmer Rouge's most hideous butchers, writes: 'As a fighting force, the Khmer Rouge no longer existed, but former members were everywhere: as government officials, army generals, village leaders. As one Cambodian put it, "They are all around us; we live among the tigers."'

But it didn't stop me being endlessly curious and the thought always lingered in the back of my mind: what army had they fought in? And, once you started asking questions, the monks quickly fell into stories of war, fighting, bloodshed. They were carriers of story, and those stories were inconceivably horrible. Talking to them I could see the truth of what Vann Nath, an artist who recorded the hideous torture inflicted on Cambodians at the infamous Tuol Sleng prison in Phnom Penh, said: 'The legacy of the Khmer Rouge lives on today—in the separated families, the orphans, the thousands of haunted, wounded people.' These monks, slender and watchful as they smoked cigarettes and squatted in their thin orange robes, were indeed haunted.

What they had lived through was impossible for me, with my life of privilege and peace, to even imagine. They had existed in a time of no culture, no religion and not even any medicine. I have been stunned to read over the years of the wilful stupidity of the Khmer Rouge ruling machine, who were unequipped to provide even the basics of civilised existence. In Khmer Rouge hospitals, untrained nurses were, according to journalist Joel Brinkley, 'injecting patients with Pepsi or coconut milk'.

The younger monks at Wat Koh were mostly from the provinces, smooth-skinned and improbably muscular young men with bright eyes, cheeky smiles and curious minds. Smuggling me into the quarters was one of their great games, and I would be seated in the corner and treated like a pet. I didn't mind. I had nothing else to do.

One of the other activities on the monastery grounds was an English conversation club, which lasted all afternoon. Local university students would gather and chat in broken English. To be honest I tended to avoid this. I know it was churlish of me, but the conversations were always painful and stilted, the same five or six questions asked over and over whenever someone new arrived.

But one afternoon, bored and desperate for company, I wandered over to the big shady tree with its concrete benches scattered below. There was the usual gathering of students, all of them impeccably dressed (at that stage most universities in Phnom Penh required a uniform— some still do) and terrified at my presence. Conversation rolled along at the pace of molasses, and I was at the point of desperation when a quiet young man appeared. He was tall and in profile exceptionally beautiful, with curly hair which, though more common in Cambodia than elsewhere in Asia, was still unusual enough to make me notice.

Aware of my look, he turned to face me and smiled. Seeing him face on, it was all I could do to stifle a gasp. I am certain my eyes must have expressed my shock and even revulsion: the exquisitely handsome right side of his face was balanced by a hideously scarred left side. His left nostril was torn away and the lip under it ripped jaggedly. A pitted scar ran all the way up to his left eye, which was pulled down into an unusual angle. 'Hello monsieur,' he said, smiling in his strange way and reaching out a hand. 'My name is Pek.'

Pek and I chatted, and I was charmed by him. I suppose my interest was flavoured with pity, and a certain condescending fascination that someone so unfortunately disfigured should also be smart, sweet and funny. He was a university student studying French and English literature. A country boy, he had come to Phnom Penh and was living with his rich Chinese aunt over by the Independence Monument. This aunt was a stall holder at Central Market, at one of the elegant raised booths right in the middle of the market. And so began my strange familiarity with this most iconic building in Phnom Penh. Pek casually asked what hotel I was staying at, and I blithely told him. After half an hour or so I left and we waved at each other, both refreshed by this unusual and mutually satisfying meeting.

Pek and I quickly developed an intense, even romantic, relationship, though it was entirely chaste. We would sit together stiffly on my bed and watch whatever was on TV. Pek had an insatiable taste for television, having grown up without one. He would drive me around Phnom Penh on his motorbike, taking me to the museum or to visit relatives and friends working at various shops around the city. We would eat, but I quickly learned that, because of his facial deformities, Pek couldn't take spicy food—the various mucal responses to chilli or pepper caused him severe pain.

He neglected his English conversation club and became jealous of my time and friendships with other Cambodians. He distrusted the motivations of the handsome young monks and warned me to stay away from the pagoda. One of his familial obligations was to work a few shifts a week at his aunt's stall at the Central Market, a huge Art Deco pile in the centre of Phnom Penh, and he insisted I accompany him. And so I sat incongruously on the raised platform behind the elegant antique wood and glass cabinets selling silver Buddha statues and huge penises carved from bone. It was an eclectic collection of objets d'art, and in those days business was not very brisk. The stall holders here sat right next to each other, with no physical barrier marking their stall out from the one next to it. I would regularly stray over into a neighbour's stock, but this was an accepted practice, and if you sold one of your neighbour's knick-knacks you would get a cut of the resulting profit.

I was, of course, a great object of fascination to the neighbouring stallholders. As I sat uncomfortably on a tall stool, one by one they would come by to see me and pepper me with questions. Being inveterate retailers, they were all multi-lingual and the conversation would range freely from English into Chinese and Vietnamese, where I was comfortable, and even into French and Khmer, where I was entirely lost. The sweet, plump-faced old lady at the next stall would give me little gifts every time I came: a tiny tiger rendered in silver; a beautiful little Buddha carved in wood; a minute Kwan Yin made from bone. I still have all of these charms. 'You are such a good man,' she would say, cupping my face with her soft hand. 'To be so kind to this poor, luckless boy. To give him your attention. You make him so happy. Just look at his terrible face,' she said, switching to Vietnamese to save his feelings, though he knew exactly what she was saying. 'He will never find a wife. I pity him.'

Pek seemed oblivious to these public displays of pity, which he attracted as a matter of course. Being hideously disfigured was not at all uncommon in Cambodia in the 90s, a country more literally scarred by war and internal conflict than any other. But when he and I were alone we would never, ever talk about the way he looked. And I had been brought up never to ask difficult or personal questions, even if I was burning with curiosity. And so I never knew what had happened to him.

Cambodians set great store in friendship. One of their favourite folk tales is that of Khvak and Khven, a blind man and a cripple who combine forces to become rich and powerful. The sharp-eyed cripple is carried about on the back of the strong and dogged blind man, and together they are unstoppable. I frequently saw statues of the two in temple courtyards, where their little moral tale made them the perfect allegorical figures.

Frustrated by wavering insistence on walking up and down that useless street, and bored by my slightly lost and vacant state, Mak finally said, 'This is boring, chasing after some ghost in your past. Let's go to Olympic Market.' Olympic Market was always where we went when were bored or hot. In fact, it wasn't the market we were visiting at all. We would walk straight by it, down through the multitudinous pharmacies and past furniture shops till we reached a section of town that seemed to specialise in soft drinks, beer and dry goods.

In this stretch, trucks big and small would load themselves with all kinds of mysterious produce—one day it was an entire load of plastic rocking horses—and head off to provincial cities. Our unlikely hang was a truck stop cafe, the kind of place that sold cheap food and iced drinks to the hot and exhausted transport workers. The proprietor was a thin Chinese man with a nasty black dog that would always lunge at me. He knew exactly six words each in English, Vietnamese, Mandarin and French, and it was on this basis that we would converse for great lengths of time. Our chats were normally over the daily paper, a particularly sensationalist broadsheet that he read carefully throughout the day. It was safest if we stuck to the pictorial section in the middle, which offered a weird collection of salacious and funny pictures stolen from the internet and affixed with Khmer captions. Elephants holding babies, monks doing bad things, men swallowing snakes—these were the items that delighted us both, and once we'd finished our analysis the pictures would be passed around to the assorted truck drivers and manual labourers who sat about the cafe shirtless, drinking cheap iced tea. This man became my friend, and he would bounce with excitement whenever I returned from a few days out of town. I met his children, though never his wife. I shared his home—he lived in the cafe when it was closed late at night—and we shared some intimacies in the thirty words we could converse in.

My Cambodian friend told him the story of my fruitless search, and all of the cafe listened in. The truck drivers, the load carriers, the delivery boys from the provinces, all nodded quietly and added their opinions and suggestions, their eyes filled with sympathy.

And it occurred to me that all of these people had lost friends and loved ones in much more tragic and hopeless circumstances. But they showed nothing but warmth and concern about my plight. Perhaps this shared experience connected all of us, showed us that everyone, in poverty or in privilege, loses someone important. All of these men had lost a friend, and my own loss had somehow put us all on an equal footing.

A GATHERING OF MONKS

The squat, dark and bass-voiced young monk had invited me to a little event he was organising. 'Just a quick thing I have arranged at the Buddhist Institute,' he said. 'It would be so nice if you could come.' When I agreed, he arranged for someone to collect me and was very pedantic about me writing down the correct date, time and location. 'We'd all be so pleased to see you at our small gathering,' he said charmingly.

The casual nature of the invitation and the fact that when I travel I resolve never to say no to any invitation, caused me to accept, though I had grave misgivings. From experience I knew that official Buddhist events in Asia could be ghastly affairs, with long speeches in languages I did not understand. They were also opportunities for me to make multiple social gaffes. But the monk's charming and offhand invitation lulled me into thinking it would be a casual affair that I could duck into and out of, so I duly noted it down in my calendar.

When the day arrived I had decided to dress a notch above my usual slovenliness. I was aware that this was a monastic gathering, and that it was at Phnom Penh's rather palatial Buddhist Institute, and the small measure of social propriety that still rests in my weary conscience forced me to wear a button-up shirt and my best pair of jeans. In truth, I had nothing more respectable in my suitcase.

As we approached the building I became rather disturbed to see that the institute's main reception hall was overflowing with monks, hundreds of them buzzing away as they greeted each other, constantly throwing the ends of their orange robes over their shoulders, or pulling the cloth more tightly against their bodies to avoid unseemly slippage.

Vibol, the event's organiser and the man who had invited me, came running down the stairs to greet me. 'You have come!' he cried, grabbing me by the hands in a most casual and un-monk-like fashion. 'This way, sir, everything has been organised for you.' This talk of organisation made me instantly wary. How much organisation had my presence at this 'casual gathering' required?

But this gathering was becoming increasingly less casual by the second. Entering the hall I saw a massive banner declaring the celebration of World Human Rights Day, one of those days declared by the United Nations that Cambodia tends to celebrate as a public holiday. I had wondered why everyone wanted to meet for lunch today, and I was already regretting the beers I'd had with my friends a couple of hours before.

One side of the vast hall was taken up with monks, young and old, wearing the subtly shifting shades of Buddhist robe, some reflecting sectarian provenance, others reflecting nothing more than an eye for fashion. Robes come in a variety of fabrics and colour in Cambodia, though all fell within a limited palette, starting at day-glo orange and ending in a deep purple. At the very front row sat the Patriarch of Cambodian Buddhism, an elderly fellow with a quick smile and a demure but still present twinkle in his eye.

The other side was taken up with lay people, male and female. The front row was politicians and the miscellaneously ennobled, who are numerous in Cambodia and have a lot of time on their hands. The next row was movie stars and singers, and there at the end was an empty seat that I realised, long before it was explained, was intended for me. All of the men were sweating in suits, and all the women dressed in crisp white blouses and exquisite silken sarongs. I glanced down at my thoroughly disreputable outfit, hardly different from what I'd wear on an inter-city bus, and my heart sank.

I was slowly, painfully introduced to all of the VIPs, the monks first. I was at home with monks, though I winced when I was described as 'the famous Buddhist writer', all the time conscious of the smell of beer on my breath. When it came time to meet the non-religious I was a mess, recklessly screwing up the complex system of *sampeah*, the pressed hand greetings that are raised higher or lower according to the status of the person you are being introduced to. I'd almost certainly offended a whole host of 'excellencies'—as every second person I met was addressed—with my clueless hand gestures. The showbiz folk were easier, many of them proffering a hand to be shaken, Western style.

Taking my ridiculously elevated place, the monk Vibol rushed over and squatted by me. 'No problems, sir, everything has been organised. You will be giving us a quick speech on Buddhism and human rights. Not to worry—whatever comes to mind. People just want to hear you.' I glanced around me in a wild panic, and crossed and uncrossed my legs, trying to hide the scuffed and dusty shoes I'd so casually thrown on. I had been lured here under false pretences, a lamb to the slaughter. I was about to make a fool of myself in front of a couple of hundred of Cambodia's most powerful people.

Noticing my discomfort, Vibol smiled and placed a comforting hand on my shoulder. 'Oh don't worry,' he said. 'You are a clever and educated man. You will have no problems speaking to us on this subject. Besides, it's just a couple of words, that's all.'

'How long, exactly?' I asked, hoping that I might escape with a warm greeting and a few clichés about how much I respected Buddhism and Cambodia's place in the world.

'Not long at all,' responded the monk. 'I've got you down for twenty minutes.'

'But that's impossible!' I said. 'I can't speak on such a complex subject unprepared. You really must excuse me from speaking—can't someone else do it?'

The monk looked worried for a fraction of a moment, but his smile returned as he regained his natural confidence in my abilities. 'Oh, you exaggerate,' he said. 'You'll be fine. Besides, it's really only ten minutes—someone will translate you after each sentence.' The thought of this added complexity made me even more terrified, and I began to sweat like crazy.

The event began, and we stood up through Cambodia's unexpectedly long national anthem and then for an even longer official Buddhist anthem. Then someone sang a long-ish patriotic song, all while we continued standing. Finally we relaxed, though my mind was racing through a million possibilities on that subject I'd never in my lifetime given even a moment's consideration: Buddhism and human rights. Everyone was up on their feet again as the Patriarch took the platform, and then down again for a politician, a millionaire and a movie star. These were all pretty substantial speeches, and I was hoping that by the end of them all there would not actually be any time left for my appearance.

As the movie star was headed into the final forty-five minutes of his off-the-cuff speech, the harried MC came running down the aisle. 'Are you ready, professor? You are on next.'

'I'm not a professor,' I said, causing the MC to check his script in an annoyed fashion.

'It says here you are,' he insisted. 'Anyway, it doesn't matter. Makes you sound better. You don't have a jacket you could wear?'

'No,' I apologised. 'I had no idea I'd be speaking . . .' The pained expression crossed his face again, and the small school boy in shorts and long socks that was standing with him giggled.

'Where's my translator?' I demanded, deciding to take an offensive stand to regain some of my dignity.

'Here,' said the MC, pushing forward the skinny child. I had a sinking feeling that we were designated to be the novelty act. Was I going to be asked to play the harmonica next? In the thunderous applause that followed the end of the actor's speech, I began to rise out of my seat with great trepidation. The young woman who had been assigned my protector beamed up at me as a bank of lights were being wheeled into place in front of the stage and a handful of cameramen began to position themselves.

'So exciting,' she said, guiding me into the aisle towards the front of the auditorium. 'We have just discovered your speech is going to be televised,' she whispered into my ear, leading me up the stairs to the platform. Taking my place behind the lectern, almost delirious from fear and anxiety, she handed me a plastic bottle of water and, just before she left me alone, she told me her final, delicious, piece of news.

'And it's going out live!'

THE TRUCK DRIVER
AND HIS GHOST

The day after my disastrous speech, I was scheduled to take my first ever trip to Battambang, Cambodia's second city, some 300 kilometres northwest, and five hours in a cramped local bus from Phnom Penh. I had already been a month in the city, and almost every time I headed down to get a bus ticket I would flick open one of the local papers and the front page story was invariably something like: HORROR BUS SMASH—5 DEAD. The Khmer-language papers were worse, featuring full-colour photos of the mutilated bodies and the ruined buses, cars and motorcycles. Cambodia was going through an epidemic of traffic accidents, and wizards, shamans and miscellaneous fortune tellers across the country were busy selling charms, talismans and special lucky pendants that would guarantee people safe passage. The drivers were fleeing the scenes of these crashes, fearing being murdered by mobs of angry bystanders.

The morning I was scheduled to leave for Battambang, my travelling companion Panit arrived bright and early at my room, brandishing that day's edition of the most lurid newspaper. 'Happened again,' he stated cheerily. 'Six dead in devastating crash on the road to Sihanoukville. One of them a foreigner!'

'Perhaps we shouldn't go,' I said, my eyes lingering on the two-page spread of horrific photographs.

'Are you mad!' said Panit, his eyes flashing with fear. 'My mother has been preparing for us for days. Besides, nothing will happen to us—I have this.' He lifted his T-shirt to expose a piece of plaited white cotton wrapped around his waist. This was his own magical belt, a thing he often invoked when embarking on any act of reck-lessness. I remembered that one of its most important functions, often described, was full protection against automobile accidents. 'I have this, and as for you, you are a good man—you don't have any karma to be involved in a bus crash. Quickly, get packed—we leave in half an hour.'

The bus station was a kind of clichéd third-world horror story, dense with beggars, women with babies, and huge piles of stuff to be transported by the buses as they crossed the country. With no functioning domestic postal service, Cambodians rely on the buses to take even small things to their families in the provinces. Panit regularly sent fruit, photographs, clothes and even money to his family in the hills surrounding Battambang using the bus post. It was up to him to call them and tell them to be at the bus station at the right time to collect their packages.

Each private bus company had their own depot, and Panit was under strict instructions to use only the Capitol bus station. 'The company is owned by an Excellency,' he explained, 'so the buses are never pulled over by the police. Plus they are the safest. You never see their buses in the newspapers.' He had been there earlier to purchase tickets, guaranteeing us a place towards the front of the bus. Cambodians despised travelling at the back of the bus which was, Panit explained, 'hot and dangerous'. Later in my trip when I travelled the country extensively by bus, I would watch men stand and argue for hours with the ticket sellers, trying to get themselves a place at the front.

The trip out of the city was uneventful and, compared to the horrors of bus travel in Vietnam, surprisingly comfortable. Panit sat by me chattering excitedly about the things we'd do once we were in Battambang until the driver slipped on a DVD of a 1990s Hong Kong kung fu movie dubbed into Khmer, after which everyone fell silent. We were soon out of Phnom Penh and driving through the sparsely populated countryside of Cambodia.

I must have drifted off to sleep, but was woken by screams and cries and the ominous stillness of the bus. My first thought was, 'Oh no—we've been in a crash.'

But, looking around me I saw that all was in place and, glancing out my window, saw that we were pulled up safely by the side of the road, on the approach to a bridge, just outside a small township. Nonetheless the screams continued, both inside and outside the bus, and everyone was streaming forwards, pushing out of the bus's doors. There was no sign of Panit. Perhaps we had been hit?

As no-one was taking any notice of me and everyone was trying to get out of the bus as quickly as possible, I thought it prudent to join the fray. There could be a fire, I worried, or a flat tyre. I was quite terrified, having been woken into an instant adrenaline rush of panic and alarm, barely even knowing where I was. Stumbling down the steps, I was met by Panit rushing towards me from the opposite direction. 'You mustn't come any further, brother, it is too terrible.'

'What is it?' I asked. 'Has there been a crash?'

'People dead,' he answered. 'Horrible things you don't want to see. Get back on the bus.'

'Were we in the crash?' I asked.

'No, but it happened just in front of us. We have to stop because we cannot get past. I told you we were on the right bus. This crash happened just a moment before us.'

Scared of being the sole white face in a scene of panic, I dutifully, and perhaps with an element of cowardice, climbed back on the bus. But Panit's wish that I be protected from the carnage was hopeless because I realised, turning to look through our bus's windscreen, that I had a panoramic view of the crash. There, right in front of me, was the wreck of a truck, its cabin torn in half so that the driver's knees were exposed to the air, no steering wheel or chassis to conceal him. His body sat there, clothes neat, his hands resting calmly at his side. Next to him was nothing but a bloody mess where the passenger had been. Scanning up, I saw that the neat and composed body of the poor driver was headless.

Later I read it had been a collision between a tour bus and a truck, each trying to get over the narrow bridge before the other, in the usual game of chicken played by heavy vehicles on Cambodian roads. The impact that had beheaded the truck driver and torn away most of his cab had also killed his two young passengers, and I couldn't help but think of them. Truck drivers' attendants are always cheery, heavily muscled young men from the provinces who often cruise the highways with their bare feet slung out the window. They were always smiling, cheeky, keen to catch the eye of a passing foreigner to have a bit of a laugh.

'Pray, brother,' said Panit, pushing me away from where I was frozen in horror at what I saw. 'Don't look at these poor people.' Soon we were on our way, our bus edging through the wrecks, the single tyres and small huddles of wailing people. Panit was quiet as we gained speed on the road towards Battambang. Finally he turned to me and said, 'That man, that driver, no head.

I fear he will become a ghost and haunt us all.' I nodded, still stunned and completely incapable of understanding what I had just seen. I was already haunted, and would remain haunted by the thought of the smiling, goofy young offsiders, those boys whose doubles I saw on roads all over Cambodia, but were now nothing more than a bloody shadow on the seat next to the driver.

POWERFUL MEDICINE

In his village in the mountains outside of Battambang, Panit can stroll through the forest and identify every second plant as a source of medicine, actual or magical. Though he belongs to the Khmer Kandal majority, he recognised the forest as sacred in many ways, fearing certain spots and glorying in the beauty of others. His stories about the forest echoed for me the experience of legendary Australian filmmaker James Gerrand, a man who has documented Cambodia since the late 1960s. He described the attitudes of the hill tribes people of Cambodia, who would guide him through the jungle and show him 'parts of the forest that they feel are sacred in some way, and if I was just wandering through the forest, I wouldn't be aware of this whatsoever'.

When Panit and I strolled down by the village reservoirs, constructed with slave labour during the Pol Pot years and filled with as much sorrow as water, he could point to trees and vines and flowers and tell me how they are used. The whole jungle is a source of healing. I was intrigued, but still set great store by the ibuprofen and Lomotil that accompanied me everywhere. Panit scolded me for my frequent—indeed, constant—use of Western medicine. My headaches, in particular, he saw as being karmic in origin, and he said he had the perfect solution for them.

'We must drive a nail into a tree, and while we do it we will say a spell. From now on the tree will have your headaches, and nothing can change that, except that the nail should be dragged out of the tree—and we both know that is impossible.' The idea of this cure excited him, and he was convinced it would be the ultimate solution to all my ills. 'You might laugh,' he said, 'but my mother once did it, and since that day she has never suffered a headache.'

But we were kept so busy in the village, and so great was my health during that idyllic period, that we forgot all about my troublesome head and the nail in the tree. When we were back in Phnom Penh, Panit caught me dissolving some grapefruit-flavoured codeine pills in a bottle of water. He hated me to take medicine in his presence and he began to berate me. Suddenly, he remembered the promised cure, and was devastated.

'Brother,' he said, 'I have let you down. We forgot completely to put a nail in a tree, and now in Phnom Penh it is impossible. Oh, I have failed you, brother. Now you must take medicine which is bad for your body, and I fear you will die young. Next time I am in the village I promise I will do this for you, to make you better.'

And so I await that wonderful day, perhaps in the midst of the most sickening migraine, when I am at my most despairing. The pain will be lifted, my head will be clear and I will be an entirely new man. All as a nail is hammered slowly into a tree somewhere in the jungle in the hills outside Battambang.

Before we had driven up into the mountains to visit Panit's family, we'd stopped at the Battambang market to buy a selection of fresh fruit to present to his mother. The bag included such rarely seen delicacies as nashi pears and imported grapes. That evening, as I was settling into my wooden bed in the big room that was their house, Panit sat on the porch outside with his mother and father eating the fruit with much noisy delight.

The next day he explained that when he was young he had searched the forest constantly, trying to find sweet fruits to bring home to his mother. 'Once,' he said, 'in the jungle, I found a beautiful, bright-red fruit I had never seen before. I brought it home to my mother and together we ate it. It smelled so good and was so sweet—completely delicious. But by that night we were both almost dead, nearly unconscious with fever. My father had to drive us both to the hospital on his motorbike. Years later, my little brother came home proudly from the forest one day clutching that same fruit. My mother recognised it instantly and took it from him and threw it in the fire.'

Throughout Panit's life his mother had been in a debt cycle, trying to keep her children in school. As a cost-saving device, Panit had been sent as a child to live as a domestic at a Buddhist temple a hundred kilometres away, high up on the mountainside. Here he could study for free and work off his debt at the monastery. One by one, his other brothers were ordained, and all of them moved to Thailand, where monks could bring in good money to be sent home to parents eking out a subsistence living in the village with their small herd of cows.

The monastery in Panit's village was a very humble affair indeed, a collection of wooden shacks in an over-grown field. We drove there on the back of a tractor, taking gifts of cakes, candy and hot flavoured milk that we had bought at one of the village stores. The young abbot and the single boy novice, the monastery's only two residents, sat on a high wooden bench and ate the snacks quickly right in front of us as we sat on mats on the ground. I had never seen monks eat food immediately after it had been given to them, and with such relish. 'They were hungry, brother,' explained Panit as we left. 'This is a poor village and sometimes no-one brings them food. If it gets too bad they have to go to the village headman and ask him to draw up a roster for people to feed them. Life is not easy for monks in a small temple like this.'

He went on to explain that this particular temple was ill-favoured by locals because of its patchy past. 'It used to be haunted,' he told me. 'At night everyone could see lights coming from the temple, though there is no electricity. It was as though the sky was shining a spotlight onto the place, night after night. At first we thought it was a good sign, but everyone knew the old monk who was living there at the time was not good. Finally the village magician received a message from heaven—the lights were a warning to us that the monk was evil.

'So the next night, when the lights began to shine down from the sky right on the monk's house, we all walked over there and made him leave. He took just a few things and walked into the jungle, but we discovered how wicked he was from what he left behind. In his room he had a TV and DVD player, which he ran on a battery, and right next to them was a box full of porno movies. Hundreds of them! The wicked old thing. By breaking the Buddha's rules he angered the gods, and so they exposed him.'

The specialty dish of Panit's mountain village was a delicately flavoured marijuana soup, and this was served to me every evening, leaving all of us pleasantly mellow and guaranteeing a good night's sleep. The sleeping arrangements were traditional, though slightly disconcerting for a Western visitor. Up in the main part of the wooden house on stilts there were two beds. The best and largest was vacated for my exclusive use. It was situated right by a window, so I could be guaranteed a breeze. The second was for Panit, because he was a beloved son returned home for a visit. His parents slept on the floor beneath us, having offered up the best positions to their guests. This was a Khmer tradition I had encountered in the Kampuchea Krom districts in Vietnam as well, but it always left me uneasy. I was conscious of my host's discomfort on the floor, though for them the situation was perfectly natural, and any other way could not be imagined.

After dinner, in the incredible black of a mountain village with no electricity, various curious villagers would emerge out of the night to sit on the edges of the weak light spread by a battery-operated LED lamp. Everyone spoke Khmer while I stretched out on the big communal wooden bed beneath the house. Periodically, people would scoot closer to peer at me and to grab some part of my body that interested them. One evening, a village tough, who had, of course, spent a period working in Thailand and was a local wit, made a series of improper comments about me, encouraged by the consumption of rice spirits, all of them translated by a laughing Panit. He speculated how I would crush any bride, hence my previously inexplicable bachelor status, and then he went on to guess how much various parts of my body might weigh, each time grabbing the part in question and testing its heft in his own hands. My hand and forearm, my belly on its own, my head, all were discussed in some length by the assembled.

Hoisting one of my legs up onto his shoulder, he let it sit there and paused thoughtfully. 'These legs—they are bigger than any of our cows' legs. One of these could feed my entire family for a week. Thirty kilos at least.' The people sitting around all murmured in agreement, variously drunk or stoned.

YON

When we were visiting Panit's village in the mountains, his mother had given me a special sacred cloth that the Cambodians call a *yon*. These are popular talismans in Cambodia, and this one was said to contain special power, having been bought from a faith healer and magician in Siem Reap. The use of protective talismans is an ancient practice in Cambodia. Elizabeth Becker, a lifelong commentator on Cambodia, writes about how the sad soldiers fighting the Khmer Rouge in the early 70s 'relied on Buddhist talismans and magic scarves for protection'.

'It brings you luck,' said Panit's mother. 'And it will protect you, from bullets and traffic accidents, and also . . . the bad intentions of love-struck women. I think you will find it valuable.' She folded it carefully into a little square and carefully again into a small green plastic bag. 'You can keep it with you at all times, in your bag or in the top pocket of your shirt. But you must never disrespect it.'

And so I have it with me to this day, always kept in my bag. Once I took it out and showed it to a Vietnamese friend, who became scared and agitated as I unfolded it. 'Cambodian magic!' he said, worried. 'Don't bring Cambodian magic around me.'

'But it's for good,' I assured him. 'It protects me.'

'Probably some spell on it to make you fall in love with a girl,' he said.

'On the contrary,' I said, 'it protects me from that very thing.'

He could only be calmed down when he saw that the pink cotton cloth had printed on it an image of the Buddha.

I had long been interested in *yon*: magical pieces of cloth the size of a handkerchief, created by monks, shamans or magicians that serve as lucky charms, talismans and protective devices. Panit's mother kept two precious *yon* wrapped in plastic high on a ceiling beam. They were both painted on light blue cloth, and were the work of a famous magician who lived in the grounds of a temple in Siem Reap. Each of the *yon* served a specific purpose. One was a marital aid—whoever was in possession of it could guarantee the fidelity and adoration of their partner. The other was a more general piece of supernatural protection. 'To protect us from bullets,' said Panit's mother. 'And also snake bite, traffic accidents, murder plots and the misdirection of malicious magical energy.' I admired both the *yon*, with their intricate patterns, drawings and inscriptions.

Hearing of my interest the next day, Panit's taciturn old uncle, who lived next door, dashed back to his house and came back brandishing his own little collection of magical materials and devices. These were *yon* on cloth and paper, some engraved bones, and a small metal cylinder that contained magical pieces of text. The uncle's collection was legendary in the village, for he had been an army man, and these items had travelled with him onto the battlefield. His very presence in the village today was testament to the efficacy of his magical items. He showed them to me with great solemnity and barely concealed pride.

'Very dangerous things,' he said, casually. 'One day I will burn them. They must never be allowed to fall into the hands of others. Incredibly powerful. Some have been adorned with corpse oil. All are possessed of their own spirits. Fortunately I can keep them in check.' He re-wrapped the collection with great care and said, 'But I am playing with fire. They served their purpose and kept me alive. I should have released them years ago. But I feel connected to them somehow—they are a part of me.' Shuffling back over the fence to his farm he turned back to me and warned, 'Always respect these things, young brother. You may not believe, but believe or not, they are powerful.'

Some weeks later, Panit and I were in Sorya Mall, that great representative of all things modern in Phnom Penh. We were off, naturally, to see a 3D film; Panit saw no other form of cinema as worthy of attending. The young man who sold us tickets at the cinema had perfectly arranged hair, emulating a popular Korean pop star. It was elegantly dishevelled, and the top had been rendered a light brown. Panit glared at him pointedly, and as we walked away I asked why he'd been so impolite to the perfectly sweet attendant. 'It is not appropriate for Cambodian people to dye their hair,' he said.

'Why on earth not?' I asked.

'Cambodia is a poor country,' he explained, astonished that I didn't understand. 'Dying your hair is a vanity, it is frivolous. It might be OK for Westerners and Koreans—they've got money and time for hair dye. But when he does it he brings shame on his mother and on his country.'

I was to hear over and over again the injunction to think of one's mother before one did anything pointless, foolish or unduly sensual. It seemed that every Cambodian had, lurking in the back of their mind, a poor, sacrificing mother who had food stolen from her mouth each time someone went on a drinking spree, visited a nightclub or had their hair done. It was my habit to visit the blind masseurs who had a small shop near my house. Once, I invited a Cambodian friend to come with me, but he looked at me, shocked. 'The whole time I would be thinking of my mother!' he said. Every wasted dollar is considered a direct theft.

Just before we went in to the cinema, Panit had a call, and checking the screen of his phone he said, 'Strange— it's my uncle. Why on earth would he be calling me? He never calls me.'

There followed a brief but incredibly animated conversation, and occasionally Panit would turn to me with eyes like saucers and run his hand over the hair on his arms—a sign that something spooky was happening. When he had finished he grabbed me and said, 'Brother—so strange you should be with me right now. My uncle is burning his *yon*—he said the time had come. He has been visited in his dreams by the spirits, and they mentioned you, and how you had been a sign of their release. He had called me especially to inform you that he has now done his duty. Things were dangerous, you see. There was the potential of these powerful spirits escaping and possessing the bodies of other people in the village.'

Panit was delighted that this had all happened so perfectly, that it had been arranged for me to be right there as it was all reported via telephone. He was smiling and shaking with nervous energy. 'Powerful spirits, brother! Capable of so much terror and horror. Oh, it makes the hairs on my arms stand up!' He was transported with delight at the sheer spookiness of it all.

I had learned to not to laugh at such statements, or to launch into a rationalist lecture about the absence of spirit realms. Friends spoke casually of spectral presences, of visitations by dragons and angels, of possession and trance. I was willing to believe in the possibility, if not the fact. When faced with this possible alternative existence I felt only curiosity and a willingness to indulge in the possible wonder of multiple worlds.

Driving me home, my *moto* driver turned against a red light and we were pulled over by two policemen lurking behind a tree. The police had just launched a new policy of actually issuing traffic tickets, rather than on-the-spot fines. It was yet to have much application, though: the notoriously corrupt police appeared unwilling to sacrifice that substantial percentage of their annual income. The plump policeman in his tight uniform and loafers scolded my *moto* and made an elaborate charade of the seriousness of his offence. The *moto* smiled and apologised softly. Fines, apparently, work on a sliding scale, and particularly scruffy and obsequious *motoduhps* have to pay much less. Mine was only charged about 50 cents, though he grumbled constantly about it once we set off again and I felt obliged to pay him for it.

I tapped on the magical *yon* in my top pocket, doubting, for a moment, its true protective powers. At least, I thought, I hadn't had a traffic accident.

THE BAYON TEMPLE

In 1996, long before the days of mass tourism to the ruins of Angkor, a surly motorcycle driver dropped me at the base of the Bayon Temple and then drove off to drink with friends for three hours. As difficult as it is to believe now, when you have to queue to get in and, on any given day, your face will be in alarming proximity to the bottom of an elderly Korean tourist climbing just above you, I was left alone at that frightening place. All alone in the early morning light, confronted by the countless faces carved into stone, all of them staring out at me.

Sacheverell Sitwell, that most feckless of aristocratic travellers, and one of the roaming literary figures that brought me to Cambodia in the first place, indulged in exactly the kind of wondering that afflicts all travellers when confronted with this peculiar place, observing how:

> Each of the huge faces has been carved in situ, and one wonders if the same sculptor carved them all; and in parenthesis whether he ever did any other work afterwards. One sculptor could be employed for ten years upon them if all the towers were ready and waiting for him to set to work. But the Bayon must have been longer than that in building, and we may think it probable that he spent his life on them.

People no longer talk about what an insane place the Bayon Temple is. The reigning cliché is that all of Angkor is a transcendent, exquisitely peaceful site linking us to an unknown ancient world. And that is probably a fair description of the spacious and exquisitely designed Angkor Wat just up the road. But the Bayon is a different kettle of fish altogether.

Less a temple than a gallery designed by the fevered mind of a madman, it is steep and cramped, terribly dangerous with its high stairs and deadly ledges. There is no design to speak of—the immense stone faces, dozens of them, are placed higgledy-piggledy, following some maniacal plan. One wanders—and sometimes crawls—across these stone terraces gazed down upon by a man, or a supernatural being, of quite incredible beauty. He is a sensualist, this mysterious stone being, thick-lipped and chubby-cheeked, exactly the kind of man you'd like to get drunk and hang out with on a Saturday evening. Handsome, but gone to seed, and looking like he enjoys the finer things in life.

These days the Bayon is teeming with people: Koreans, Chinese, French, Singaporeans, all in unwieldy tour groups, their Cambodian guides sweating and anxious about what might happen on this unpredictable, crumbling stone pile. Were it situated in the West you wouldn't be allowed to approach it, let alone clamber over it. It is an insurer's nightmare, and I speak from experience.

In 1996, attempting to climb down one of the Bayon's as yet unrenovated stairways, a piece of stone moved under my foot and I fell, landing heavily at the bottom, some metres down. I was lucky that I hadn't hit my head, but my leg and arm were screaming with pain and my foot was just numb. And there was blood, lots of blood, seeping into the expensive white linen shirt I had thought would be just the romantic thing for a bit of tropical exploration. I felt so unutterably alone—why had I ever embarked on such a foolish, wilfully dangerous, adventure?

The guide books state confidently that the massive stone faces of the Bayon represent someone or something. The Bodhisattva Lokesvara, they say, or the King Jayavarman who had constructed the temple, or even both. But Ian Harris, historian of Cambodian Buddhism, paints a much more complicated and mysterious picture. In fact, no-one has any idea whose face is carved again and again into the stone and hoisted up high on this ridiculous structure. It might be the Buddha Sakyamuni or the future Buddha Maitreya. It might be the Bodhisattva Vajrasattva or even the Hindu god Brahma. Whoever it is, my thoughts about him are inappropriate and disrespectful in the extreme.

And on that morning I was convinced that he was witnessing my death, had perhaps even caused it. I was distracted by those lips, curled up so sensually, so full and so beautiful. Lips you could kiss. Wasn't I looking at those lips instead of at the perilous stone structure beneath my feet? Now I sat crumpled up in the rock chamber below, bleeding. No-one at all was around as the sun came up. I was left alone and I decided it was undignified for a grown man to cry in his final moments. I instead stared resolutely ahead and, appearing from a corner of the dark chamber I was lying in, there suddenly loomed my saviours.

They were unlikely angels: an elderly and very obese doctor from Kansas City wearing shorts and socks pulled up high and his partner, a muscled young Filipino. They were on a side trip from Manila, where, I discovered later, they had recently met and fallen in love. 'What the hell!' cried the doctor on seeing me, as much alarmed by my presence as concerned. Perhaps he thought I was a manifestation of the demons that seemed to haunt this place. They both rushed towards me, leaping with unexpected lightness and agility over the rocks to get to me. They sat with me and the doctor gave me a full examination. Other people began to arrive, locals who came to the temple to beg or to sell incense and flowers to the people who came to worship at the small shrines still active within the temple complex. They looked at us with fear and left quickly. The last thing they wanted was to get involved with a dead foreigner.

After an immensely kind hour comforting me and checking my various cuts and bruises, they asked if I thought I could stand and, being trained to be embarrassed by injury, I got up and found I could indeed walk. 'You're all cut up, buddy,' said the cheerful plump doctor, 'but I think you're gonna be OK. Nothing broken there.' The Filipino guy went out to buy me a Coke and eventually they left me. My driver freaked out when he returned and saw the way I looked. Though it was only eight in the morning he was stinking drunk, and he blamed himself for my injury. 'Why didn't I stay with you?' he asked again and again in a fit of drunken self-reproach. He silently drove me back to my hotel room where I lay in immense pain over the next few days, watching the bruises all over my body shift in shape, size and colour.

My driver, intent on remaining engaged at $10 a day, sat on the floor in my room watching MTV, wrapped in a blanket against the air-conditioning and bringing me sticky rice, spring rolls, sticks of barbecued meat and, once, a short and plump Chinese man, who turned out to be a masseur. He applied herbal compresses to my bruises and, with the worst ones, dug his fingers directly into the most damaged spots, making my head spin with pain. I was delirious and feverish, and fully expected both of them to rob me blind. I could have done nothing about it.

But instead my driver, a truly scary-looking man with tattoos and no teeth, took charge of my care with great seriousness. He bathed me and fed me and made sure I had water. He rubbed liniment on my bruises and stroked my head with great tenderness when I awoke moaning and crying. He tidied my room, though I tried to explain that the hotel staff did that, and basically lived with me for five days, never leaving my side. He protected me, and to this day I remain humbled by the thought of his gentleness and concern, though I don't remember his name.

After almost a week I decided I was well enough to go back to Phnom Penh, and he rode me to the airport on the back of his motorbike. The Chinese masseur turned out to be a genius. Every spot he had pressed so agonisingly was healing rapidly. At the airport my saviour driver took my hand and began to cry a little. 'I will always remember you,' he said, his sunburned, crinkly face taking on a look of gentleness. 'I worry about you so much.' His shabby shirt was missing several buttons and I could see the black tattoos etched across his wiry chest. Who was this man, I thought, what must he have experienced? He was not much older than me, but I knew that he must have lived through hell. Everyone of that age, at that point in Cambodia's history, had.

'I won't forget you either,' I said, pushing some more money into his hand. I was young and embarrassed and still a little sick. I wanted to be away from here.

'You gave me too much money,' he mumbled, pushing the dollar bills into his pocket shyly. Grabbing me again, he pulled me close to him and his eyes filled with tears.

'I love you,' he said.

I giggled like the child I was and said, 'Oh goodness, aren't you sweet? Thank you for taking care of me.' I pretended I was in a great hurry, that I had to rush into the airport building, where he wasn't allowed.

'Come back to see me,' he said.

'I will,' I promised. 'How could I forget how good you've been to me?'

But I never saw him again.

SUNRISE AT ANGKOR WAT

The thing to do is go and watch the sunrise over Angkor Wat. It is a romantic notion. One stumbles across the causeway in the dark, confronted by a phalanx of attendants with linked arms ensuring you possess the requisite ticket and then abandoning you once more to the dark. You fall in with a middle-aged Chinese woman who has a torch affixed to her hat, and you wonder why no-one told you that this sort of thing would be useful. After lining up to walk through the first stone gate—why are there so many people around at this time of day?—you find yourself on a second causeway, and several small children loom out of the darkness with torches and say, 'Breakfast, sir? Banana pancakes, coffee—the sun won't be up for an hour yet.'

So you let yourself be ferried away to one of the food concessions outside one of the modern Buddhist temples that sit at the sides of the ancient one. Here omelettes and toasted baguettes and Ovaltine are prepared on small wood fires, and there really aren't all that many other people at the restaurants and you begin to think, 'This is more like it, this is an adventure.'

But then the sun comes up and slowly it emerges. No, not the ancient wonder of Angkor Wat, a place that so many have said must be seen before you die. The truly remarkable sight is the slowly materialising vision of hundreds of other tourists scattered about, great crowds of them with tripods and cameras, all of them aiming for that special shot. It is one of the most incredible sights in the modern world—what the hell are all these people doing in Cambodia?

Unless you aim upward, it is almost impossible to get an unsullied shot of the ruins, so numerous and unpredictable are the crowds. And it doesn't help that, for a couple of years now, parts of the temple have been covered in blue tarps and scaffolding, part of the endless and ongoing restoration and conservation of this site. Paul Theroux says that, more than deadly beasts or warfare, what every traveller fears most is the presence of other travellers, and that fear must be confronted head-on on one's first morning in Angkor. You are instantly reminded that you are no longer special or uniquely adventurous.

The foremost historian on Cambodia, David Chandler, calls Angkor Wat 'a coded religious text that could be read by experts moving along its walkways from one dimension to the next. The learned people that designed the dimensions of Angkor Wat would have been aware of and would have revelled in its multiplicity of meanings.' This multiplicity tends to be reduced on any crowded morning when you can't get in because of a stout German planted in the middle of the main entrance with a tripod, determined to capture precisely the mood of ancient mystery.

After several experiences of the beauty of Angkor Wat at sunrise, I vowed to try it at some other time, and so the next time I came to Siem Reap with my Cambodian friend Panit I decided to do other things in the morning and catch the most famous temple in mid-afternoon. I figured that by 2 p.m. it would be so dazzlingly hot that not even the most intrepid photographer would be able to bear it. So instead we whiled away our time at some of the deservedly less popular spots, though no matter how paltry the ruin, a souvenir seller or three would manage to emerge from the jungle and apply their tenacious sales pitch to us.

We made our way to the Khmer Culture Club restaurant, a pleasant enough tourist joint in Angkor that must offer serious kickbacks to tuk tuk drivers, because I have never been taken anywhere else when I suggested lunch. Panit was engrossed by the menu, which offered every food imaginable ranging across a number of cuisines. 'I think I will have a French dish, followed by a Thai dish and finish with a Khmer dish,' he declared. As we sat back and waited for our food, three young male backpackers came in, all of them looking a hot mess in singlets, shorts and flip flops. One had even opted for combat-print bicycle shorts. Panit's eyes bugged. 'Has he come in his underwear?' he asked.

While that one may have looked like he was in underwear, the young Italian in their group had opted for none at all, and was obviously going commando in his silky red soccer shorts. 'I can see his penis, clearly,' said Panit, not quite softly enough, as people at other tables giggled. But it was true. The Italian boy's bulge made something of an advance guard, and length and girth were all matters of little mystery as that part of him swung into the restaurant a good ten seconds before the rest of his body. The men were also inordinately loud, and the three of them took up the energetic, if not the physical, space of a dozen Cambodians.

Panit had taken a half-hour that morning to select the clothes he was going to wear to Angkor Wat, that proudest symbol of the Khmer people. All of the Cambodians we encountered were dressed neatly, respectfully. Marie D Jones and Larry Flaxman, in their book *11:11*, discuss the incredible evidence of a sacred geometry at work in ancient sites such as Angkor. There is a harmonic relationship that is palpable at Angkor; you feel as though you are in the presence of something significant, transcendent—something beyond the merely monumental. This kind of sacred architecture is described by the authors as 'the most profound manner by which man could somehow emulate the divine patterns of the heavens—right here on earth. Even today, these structures elicit a deep and lasting impression upon those who view them.'

But most of the young Westerners strolling through were dressed as though for a day at the beach—a bad day at that. They seemed to have no comprehension that they were touring a sacred space, frequently entering the site of active shrines, temples and places of worship. 'Why do they dress like his?' asked Panit, pained but genuinely seeking to understand. 'Would they wear such clothes in their own country?' I couldn't help but wonder. Would they dress like that while visiting, say, Notre Dame or the Duomo? Climate aside, surely even the most resolutely atheistic tourist might hesitate for a moment before deciding to wear cut-offs and a bikini top while touring St Peter's Basilica?

'When the Angkor complex was "discovered" by French missionaries and explorers in the 1850s, Angkor Wat contained a prosperous Buddhist monastery inside its walls, tended by several hundred hereditary slaves,' writes David Chandler again in his *A History of Cambodia*. To this day the complex is filled with sacred statues and shrines where people kneel to pray and offer incense, and at each side of the temple is a large and active monastery that offers toilet facilities to tourists. There is no disguising the site's religious purpose, and the great pride that Cambodians take in this amazing place.

That afternoon, as we rested on the main causeway leading into the Angkor Wat, we saw them again, the trio of scruffy young Euro-backpackers. 'Look!' I said, catching sight of the unmistakable heft of the Italian's swinging pride leading the way inside his shiny red shorts. 'Remember them?'

'Yes,' said Panit, averting his eyes towards the sacred lotus towers of this ancient temple. 'I remember them. For all the wrong reasons.'

THE CHINESE CHRONICLERS

The Cambodians have an ambiguous relationship with the Chinese journeyers who recorded their early travels there. They acknowledge their importance in being the first to actually record details of early Khmer life, but they can't help but be offended by the descriptions of themselves that go against national myths. To the Chinese, the Khmer were ugly, brutal, naked and savage. All of these things are the most tremendous insults to the Khmer. There was a wax effigy of one of these Chinese observers at the Cambodian Culture Village in Siem Reap and Panit sneered when he looked at it and said, 'He was a liar.'

The Cambodian Culture Village is a large and entirely awful 'amusement' park on the outskirts of Siem Reap, constructed, one supposes, to provide some kind of context to the actual ruins of Angkor twenty minutes further away. I suspect that the village had once enjoyed glory days, and almost every young Cambodian you meet will tell you of a pleasure-filled school excursion to Siem Reap which culminated in a thrilling visit to the Cambodian Culture Village. Those days seem long gone, however, and now the park is dusty, empty and very much down-at-heel.

Having paid the extortionate entry fee and walked by the two heavily armed door guards, we were ushered into a darkened hall featuring a series of dioramas depicting key moments in Cambodian history. I had seen such dioramas before, and they held no interest for me. What did preoccupy me was the industrial-strength air conditioner roaring above the entrance. Panit and I found ourselves shouting at each other instead of conversing, and we realised that the hissing, spitting and throbbing air conditioner was deafening us both. It had also chilled the room to sub-zero temperatures and Panit's body began to shake with cold, though he insisted on paying full and careful attention to each dusty diorama. The little signs explaining each display were written in Khmer and Chinese only, a fact which managed to infuriate Panit. 'No English at all,' he grumbled. 'How do they expect tourists to come here?'

Once we were back out into the main park we were soon baking in the forty-plus degree heat, though this climatic swerve did little to sway Panit's enthusiasm.

The vast concrete boulevards led to small grassy knolls that contained miniature versions of iconic Cambodian buildings, and these Panit exclaimed at. There was not a single other person in this whole huge area. We made our way through the staggering heat, covering whole kilometres, skirting monstrous restaurants and massage halls. We were the only figures, shimmering in the heat, me on the verge of collapse.

Eventually we found the recreated ethnic villages, and here there was some sign of life. A few aged women were trying to sell overpriced soft drinks and bowls of Khmer noodles from street carts. Stages were erected for the purposes of recreations of village life, including one that depicted a savage tribe that Panit assured me were well-known cannibals. But the show times were all hours away, and not even Panit showed any willingness to hang about to see one. One or two Cambodian families were here, sitting about in the shade and slight cool provided by a fake lagoon. The looks on their faces were tragic, having spent so much money to come to a place so completely lacking fun. Panit started to talk to a couple and their complaining young children. 'They are telling me the whole place is a waste of time,' he said sadly. 'It's a ghost village more than a culture village. I feel pity for them—they are a poor family from the provinces and they have spent all their money on coming here.'

Next to a huge cage filled with howling gibbons, there was a large fake cement mountain outside which hung a banner saying: 'Judgement Tunnel'. The banner was washed red with blood, and had a few tantalising images of ravaged corpses and toothy demons with human entrails spilling from their mouths. This looked like fun. 'Let's go in here,' I said, keen to see just what was in store inside the Judgement Tunnel.

Peeking in through the entrance at the base of the concrete mountain we saw nothing but a darkened cavern. No-one was inside and no-one was outside to check our tickets or to explain what the hell was going on. Panit quickly pulled his head out of the room. 'Brother, I suggest you don't want to go in there,' he said.

'Why on earth not?' I said. 'It looks like great fun—like a ghost ride.'

'That's exactly it,' said Panit, a great believer in the supernatural. 'Nothing inside but ghosts and demons and horrible images of the pits of hell. Nothing we want to see, especially with nobody else around.'

'But that's exactly what I want to see,' I answered, knowing that this might be the only redeeming feature of this ghastly tourist trap. So I ducked in and Panit, fearing for my safety, followed after me, complaining loudly from the very moment he entered.

'Oh, this is truly terrible—we don't know what we are going to see here. I beg you brother, leave now!' But I doggedly made my way through the rooms as they progressed deeper into the bowels of the cement mountain. 'Notice that we are descending?' said Panit, his eyes bulging. 'What a cruel person invented this place. I fear I cannot continue with you.'

In truth, the horrors of the Judgement Tunnel were tame indeed, made up of the carnival tricks that any rider of a ghost train has endured in their childhood. Passing through doors hung with fake hair in the deepest dark, we would stumble upon a suddenly illuminated papier-mâché demon tearing a mannequin in two. Each time Panit would scream in genuine terror, and as we progressed I had to physically drag him through the descending doorways. 'This is too much for a country boy,' he said. 'What terrible mind devised this?'

The various torments of Buddhist hell were depicted in vivid, glowing 3D, each chamber devoted to evoking the visceral sufferings of the wicked and sinful. In one a naked person climbed a thorny tree, leaving a bloody trail of torn flesh and dripping internal organs. The root cause of his punishment was carefully recorded on a sign below. 'Men who sleep with the wives of others!' crowed Panit, isolating his single favourite sin. 'I told you, didn't I?' he said to me, fixing me with a triumphant smirk, pleased to have this documentary evidence of his constant warnings.

In the next room naked women, their hands bound behind them, were having their tongues torn out at the root by black-skinned demons. Around them lay their equally suffering sisters with violent green serpents suckling at their breasts, blood pouring from their nipples. Reading the accompanying explanation carefully, Panit told me that the women losing their tongues had spoken to their parents cruelly, and those nursing snakes had been fault-finders and scolds.

And then, right at the very deepest point of the Judgement Tunnel, was a spot-lit statue of the Buddha, resplendent in golden robes. Right next to him began a long and narrow staircase that led to an exit at the very top of the mountain. The doorway there shone reassuringly from the hot sun outside it. The choice was stark: we could either continue through the horrors of hell, its twisting and never-ending corridors, or we could take the quick route by the Buddha's side, straight into the safe and beautiful day.

Panit fixed me with a beseeching look. In truth there was nothing I wanted to do more than keep going through that musty, cement-smelling mountain to see just how Cambodians depicted the horrors of hellish suffering. And that stairway was narrow, steep and perilous, with no handrails. It was not designed for a man of my size. 'I will leave you if I have to,' warned Panit. 'I simply cannot continue into this place. It is horrible, I will never sleep tonight.' And at that he clambered up the stairs. On a whim I followed too, a little scared for myself in that dark cavern, all alone. It was all I could do to balance on each tiny step, and if I'd have slipped, which seemed at that moment a certainty, I would have plunged several storeys to my death, right next to the plaster-of-Paris reprobates being disembowelled for some unknown sin.

When I finally forced myself through the tiny door at the top of the mountain, Panit sat there smiling, drinking a Coke. I should have known that soft-drink sellers, that most intrepid species of retailer, would have made their way up here to trap the unwary religious. 'You made the right decision, brother,' he told me. 'My skin crawls when I think of the horrors you made me look at.'

THE PERILS OF BEING WELL READ

Cambodia is a difficult place to write about, I cannot lie. The longer I stayed in Cambodia, the less I understood it, and the more frustrated I became. I am not one of those who has fallen in love with Cambodia: it is a place too complex, too guarded and too weighed down by its own history for me to be able to embrace it. The history is everywhere, and yet is always just beyond grasp. A history that all Cambodians claim to be proud of, and yet have such a shaky grasp of when you begin to question them about it.

I suppose I was born with a doubting kind of mind. My grandfather and my mother are both famous contrarians, often to the detriment of knowledge and certainly seamless social intercourse. Their example has left me wanting to be a bit more trusting, a bit more credulous, but heavens I find it difficult. And being in Cambodia only made the distrustful side of me grow. Cambodian friends would breezily and with great assuredness tell me things that were absolutely wrong. They would attribute things to the wrong historical period, the wrong religion or the wrong language. And Cambodians are possessed of an unshakeable conviction that every single thing of any quality has its roots in Cambodia, so if I dared to praise something Thai or Vietnamese or Laotian I would be primly informed that these things were actually Cambodian and had simply been stolen, copied or misappropriated.

So I began to rely more and more on a little photocopied edition of David Chandler's wonderfully accessible history of Cambodia. Yes, I am ashamed to admit it was a pirated edition. I was stumbling about Siem Reap trying to avoid the heat, wishing I could understand anything about this strange country when there, on the table of a bookshop around the corner from the inter-city bus stop, I saw the slightly faded volume and knew the time had come to read it. For this sin against international copyright laws I beg forgiveness, and, should I ever meet Professor Chandler, I hereby solemnly promise I will slip him a couple of bucks in restitution. Can I be arrested for confessing this?

Though I'm not sure an exhaustive history of a country is the best thing to read while you are travelling around it. For starters, it turns you into an unbearable smart arse. Once, watching a historical drama on TV set in Angkorean times I turned to my viewing companion, the writer Suong Mak, and said, 'This is fun, but you know I really don't think that most of the people depicted here would have been wearing any clothes at this period in Cambodian history. Nakedness was pretty much standard then.'

Mak looked wounded. 'No! How dare you suggest the people of Angkor wandered about naked! This is a myth. In fact, the cloth woven at the time was so fine that, in the carvings, it appears as though the people were naked. But really, they were fully clothed and modestly dressed.'

This is actually the popular line in modern-day Cambodia, where most people are squeamish about the naked body and are pained by the multitudinous bare breasts carved into the temples at Angkor. This story also falls into line with the prevailing ideas that the people of Angkor were possessed of technologies that have been lost to time. The common folkloric belief was that Angkor Wat was constructed by a divine architect possessed of magical powers who modelled the temple, somewhat prosaically, on Lord Indra's ox stable. Normally I would smile and nod when I heard such an assertion, but my compulsive reading of Chandler's history had made a pedant of me, and I spent a good deal of the rest of the night poring through the book looking for references to the nakedness of the people of Angkor. And, for the record, I think I'm right.

A firm grasp of history changes forever one's views of the mystical ruins at Angkor. In an interview with the *Cambodia Daily*, Professor Chandler said that he sees Angkor Wat and the surrounding ruins as evidence, not of terrific achievement and advanced technology, but instead of political oppression. Chandler is quoted saying: 'There is no way anybody wanted to lift those stones for any reason.' And I must admit that spending a couple of hours at Angkor Wat on a hot afternoon might provide the proof of this assertion. It is a line taken up as well by journalist Joel Brinkley in his book *Cambodia's Curse*. The Western imagination has always wanted to see Angkor through the lens of art, mysticism and the romantic trope of lost civilisation. But in fact, it is more properly a testament to oppression, slavery and an impulse to religious folly on the part of a series of terrifying autocrats.

But what's most terrifying about Angkor Wat in the twenty-first century is the rabidness of the soft-drink and souvenir sellers outside. These people, the descendants of the slaves that constructed this strange collection of stone monuments, have embraced the tenets of commerce, if not bullying, in a particularly hyper way. Once, visiting Angkor Wat with my friend Panit, I made the mistake of smiling at a young drinks vendor on the way in. 'You remember me, sir!' he cried as I swept past. 'You come back out and buy from me! For sure!'

An hour or so later we were out, and Panit was thirsty and desperate for a drink. He made his way to the closest drinks seller and, while he was handing over his extortionate one dollar, we were suddenly assailed by a shrill cry: 'Fuck you! What's your problem? You promise me, you buy from me! You give me a dollar, now!' Panit addressed him in Khmer, and a noisy argument erupted. I led Panit away, though we were followed for a while by young Mr Customer Service.

Panit was fuming. 'Not only did they charge me a dollar for a drink—and me, a Cambodian!—but he tries to get more from me for some bizarre reason. We didn't even talk to that creature. And you know what the worst thing was?'

'What?' I asked, expecting a sorrowful dissection of the loss of traditional Khmer ways.

'That little shit was wearing an Angry Birds T-shirt. I hate Angry Birds.'

Panit and I had become particularly simpatico, and I was cheered to have found a genuine friendship in Cambodia, to know somebody who so readily and completely made me a part of his life. He was comfortable enough to tell me when my demands were not possible, when his real life might have to impinge on my strange traveller's existence. He had taken me to his home village to meet his grandmother, his parents, to see his cows and to visit the poor and somewhat overgrown little pagoda where he had spent his requisite years as a novice. Panit had been the first boy in his village ever to have gone to university, and to afford his trip and his first year's tuition, the villagers had all pitched in by selling a cow each and giving the money to him.

Chandler, in his history, says that the average size of a Khmer village—200 people—was the same in the 1960s as it was in Jayavarman's time in the twelfth century, and as it remains now. Certainly Panit's village in the mountains outside of Battambang had that timeless, romantic feel to it, and was probably around 200 people. The villagers lived simple, frugal existences, smoking wild-growing marijuana for pleasure in the evenings and working twelve hours a day just to keep themselves fed. But Siem Reap has developed from a collection of dismal villages into one of the fastest-growing cities in Asia. It is a boom town that is shaking off the dust of medieval rurality and embracing Korean restaurants, hip-hop clubs, boutique hotels and gay saunas. It is a town unrecognisable from the semi-rural idyll I knew in the mid-1990s.

SAIGON 2007

The Cambodians don't smoke nearly as much as their near neighbours, the Vietnamese. All of my friends in

Cambodia were non-smokers, and smoking on the streets was so rare as to be noteworthy. The only place where everyone smoked was in Saigon 2007, the dark and dingy Vietnamese-run cafe that I made my second home, where university boys who looked like primary school students chain smoked ostentatiously, trying to look bigger and stronger with each puff. The air became quite fuggy and my clothes, bag and books would have to be doused in cheap perfume to get the smell out.

I had, for a while, tried another coffee shop, a cleaner and more modern-looking one which served cold Cokes and the most delicious brownies. But this place, situated in a large and beautiful heritage villa, had only one, very small, air conditioner, and there was normally a gaggle of university students collected under it. The rest of the customers panted in forty-degree heat, several degrees hotter than the scorching streets outside. After my brownie was finished I was entirely drenched in sweat, my face glowing pink, and my books and papers damp. Saigon 2007, by comparison, was in a roomy cavern of a space, constantly dark and cool, kept cooler by the dozens of wall-mounted fans that were turned on by tugging the filthy cords that hung from them. On very hot days the boss would bring out an additional pedestal fan which would be positioned directly behind my head and turned up to full strength. After an hour my neck would be stiff with cold, but I was always too polite to ask for it to be turned off.

Problems arose during electricity blackouts, which are common in Phnom Penh. Saigon 2007 is not the kind of establishment that can afford its own private back-up generators, and in the course of a long, hot afternoon, the huge darkened room began to take on the aspect of a field hospital, or a church hall in the last days of the Apocalypse. Customers took off more and more clothing and assumed more and more horizontal positions until the floor was filled with a heaving, sweating mass of near-naked men groaning in their misfortune. Fortunately the pre-industrial conditions in the kitchen meant that the cafe could remain open for business no matter what the electrical vagaries. But if I ever attempted to gain entry during a blackout the owner's fierce nephew, a scowling and commanding young man with a huge scorpion tattooed on his right hand, would bar my way. 'You're not to come in during power failure,' he would say gruffly. 'My aunt says so. It's too dangerous.'

But I persisted in going to Saigon 2007 because the solitary traveller is always desperate to find some sort of home base, a place in which he is recognised and treated with some degree of familiarity. The amiable owner was a short, plump Vietnamese woman who staffed the cafe with her family: two beautiful and clever daughters who were at university, the aforementioned disreputable young nephew with his terrifying tattoos and an ancient mother who sat over a wood stove in a gothic kitchen at the back of the cafe, preparing the delicious coffee. The entire family always addressed me in Vietnamese, once I let on that I could speak it. But they always did so very quietly, and if our chatter ever got too loud the Cambodians at nearby tables would look at us with pained expressions.

'I try not to speak Vietnamese in public,' said the owner, her voice almost totally inaudible. 'The customers don't like it, you see. You have no idea how much the Cambodians hate us. I tried not to teach my daughters because I didn't think it was safe for them to know.' While the Cambodians seemed to harbour an almost universal hatred towards the Vietnamese, in Vietnam the Khmer are treated with a more casual kind of racism. They are seen not as threats, but more as hopeless mystics lost in the modern world. The central government of Vietnam condemns the forms of Buddhism practised in ethnically Khmer districts and says that the insularity of Khmer communities hinders their growth and modernisation. But in Cambodia the Vietnamese are viewed as colonisers, looters and destroyers of identity.

While the students who made up the bulk of her custom were treated like the children they were, the owner extended towards me an exaggerated hospitality. My peculiar and constant presence, and my knowledge of Vietnamese, made me an enormous curiosity, and a great deal of fuss was made. My table was always being wiped, my ice constantly replaced. If I were to glance up from my book or journal there would be a race to my table to see what I wanted.

The students played noisy games with the wooden sets provided by the cafe. These games were a mystery to me, but they involved a good deal of shouting. The proprietor's daughters were always pressed into service on their days off from study, and it wasn't unknown for them to slap, scold or even kick out some of the more forward boys. Cards were much in evidence too, but these were favoured by the older men who ordered in food from the nearby street stalls and sat quietly gambling with their friends, watched closely by the scorpion tattoo boy, who might have been picking up tips.

I never once saw a woman in the place, apart from the owner and her family. It was a decidedly masculine space, not at all the kind of romantic and spotlessly clean cafe favoured by young couples. In spite of this there were piles of Cambodian women's magazines, and many of the customers read the latest issues carefully, often going away from their groups to sit on their own and leaf through them. I, too, studied each new issue when it came in, though I could never understand the beautiful, looping letters of Khmer writing. The photographs themselves were telling, and frequently dramatic. Women's magazines in Cambodia don't shrink from reporting murders and suicides if they have a romantic element involved, and they graphically document acid attacks and emasculations, with pictures of the wounded and breathless interviews with witnesses.

It was at Saigon 2007 that I first met Kimly, the man who would become my stalwart friend—and occasional source of exasperation—in Phnom Penh. I don't know how I first noticed him, but I became gradually aware of his presence. Being in his late twenties, he stood out from the students. Dark skinned and slightly muscular, he was strangely handsome despite a lack of chin and a good deal of nose. He would sit alone at a table nearby and order an iced tea—the cheapest item on the menu, at just a few cents—and he would stare resolutely at the twin television screens for an hour or so during the hottest part of the morning.

I should mention here that one of the features of Saigon 2007 was its twin television screens, each played a totally separate entertainment. Normally one played a martial arts flick while the other played Khmer music videos. They were played at full volume, meaning that each could only ever really be properly heard when there was a lull in the noise of the other. I suppose it provided a variety of entertainment for different tastes. A surprising number of people, my soon-to-be friend Kimly among them, would pay careful attention to the screens, and sit watching for hours. I was never really sure if they were watching one or both. When I finally got a chance to ask Kimly, he said, 'Sometimes one, sometimes another—it doesn't get boring then. I have one criticism, though—she doesn't change the DVDs often enough.'

Kimly and I established a nodding acquaintance and sometimes, glancing up from the work I had brought to the cafe, I would catch him staring at me. Almost all the other regular customers had, after the Khmer fashion, cultivated a studious sangfroid when it came to me, and pretended I didn't exist. One day, absorbed in writing up my journal, my attention was grabbed by someone sitting at my table and plonking their drink between us. It was Kimly, who had finally drummed up the courage to say hello. 'I would like to suggest,' he said, in a surprising bass, 'that you don't work so hard. Doing work in a cafe is not usual in Cambodia.' Thrusting his hand forward he said, 'My name's Chicken. Nice to meet you.'

I baulk at calling a grown man Chicken, so I asked, 'Is that really your name?'

Kimly flashed his charming crooked-toothed smile and said, 'Of course not, but everyone calls me that because I look like a chicken. I have skinny legs, you know, and here . . .' At this point he held his hand to his long, slender throat where a prominent Adam's apple bobbed up and down. According to Cambodian aesthetics these were significantly ugly features, earning

Kimly his nickname. But by any Western measure he was undeniably attractive, with his faultless bronze skin, sparkling black eyes and geometric cheekbones. He held my gaze for a heartbeat and then he said, 'But my real name is Kimly. Wanna go somewhere?'

'Like where?' I asked, not at all worried by this invitation from a total stranger.

'I dunno,' he said, his English slangy, Americanised and quite perfect. 'Pagoda, museum, restaurant—somewhere tourists like to go.' At this I bristled. There's nothing a tourist hates more than being called a tourist.

'I don't like going places where tourists go,' I said, petulantly.

He looked confused for a moment, and then he said, 'OK, we can go somewhere that Cambodians like to go—somewhere boring.'

Agreeing to what sounded like a perfect plan, I called for the bill. As I prepared to leave, the cafe's owner came running up to me with a worried look on her face. 'Sir,' she said, whispering to me in Vietnamese, 'are you going somewhere with that young man?'

'Yes,' I said, 'he's taking me sightseeing.'

'Oh sir,' she said, worried to distraction, 'I can't vouch for that man, not at all. I barely know him—he is just a customer. Please be careful.'

Glancing over I saw the slender Kimly getting onto his motorcycle. He was easily half my weight, and a less threatening demeanour it was impossible to imagine.

'I'll be fine,' I assured her. 'I'm a great big man—nobody will bother me.'

She looked between me and Kimly, making calculations and envisioning potential horrors. 'You are far too gentle and trusting. You don't understand that this is a dangerous place. You can't just trust strangers in Cambodia.'

'I'll be fine, big sister,' I assured her. 'I am a seasoned traveller, and besides, he's a clever and educated man. He speaks perfect English.'

At this her eyes grew big and she clutched my arm. 'My God, that's worse, much worse. Bad people always speak English.' Chuckling at her concern I got up onto the back of Kimly's motorcycle and smiled as we sped off into the mean streets of suburban Phnom Penh.

THE MUSEUM AT WAT PHNOM

I don't know of any other place so oppressively lashed to its own history as Cambodia. Cambodian people, from every social level, are convinced their country was once great though, as historian David Chandler points out, 'No one knows for certain how long people have lived in what is now Cambodia, where they came from, or what languages they spoke before writing was introduced, using an Indian-style alphabet, around the third century CE.' The Cambodians have a rich mythological history, one filled with fairies and dragon kings and a population spawned by the meeting of a supernatural being with a royal human.

The historical glories of Cambodia are constantly invoked, in a way I have never noticed in other countries. The ancient temples of Angkor serve an immense psychological purpose for the Cambodians, and someone once pointed out that Cambodia is the only country in the world to feature a ruin on its national flag.

Wat Phnom sits atop a small hill and is the sacred point at which an old woman called Penh created a temple to house four divine images she discovered inside a tree trunk. Grandma Penh, as she is known, has her own very busy shrine on the top of the Wat Phnom Hill, a bust of a middle-aged woman with square spectacles and her hair in a bun. This shrine is always crowded with people offering incense, and they come to leave gifts of cheap perfume, lipsticks, swatches of luxurious fabric, new spectacles and all of the things it might be supposed an elderly lady would be desiring. It seems popular with women, though its attendant is a taciturn old fellow with deep wrinkles and a permanent scowl. Right by the shrine he has put up a number of instructional posters which always intrigued me. One in particular supplied a whole wealth of Khmer etiquette: how men and women should bow to the Buddha (a most uncomfortable on-the-toes squat for men, a position I can never assume), and the right colours to wear on particular days of the week. I was always studying the illustrated guide to *sampeah*, the act of greeting with the palms raised and joined together in front of the body as I have never properly mastered it.

The whole Wat Phnom complex, with its mysterious shrines and its constant busy-ness did seem to be a special place, a naturally energetic landmark that contained all of the dichotomies of the town that surrounded it. This place was the beginning of a city that was to become Cambodia's capital, and so was a natural site to situate a museum in. But, 'That looks like a bad museum,' I would think to myself, making my way through the hookers and glue sniffers who squatted on their haunches just outside it. My friends in Phnom Penh harboured greater hopes. 'There is an excellent museum at Wat Phnom,' people would say. 'I haven't actually visited, but I mean to. Learn all about my city.'

I have no idea how I eventually ended up there, though I know it was probably due to a combination of boredom and peer pressure, the catalyst of most of my experiences in Cambodia, or indeed anywhere in the world. I went accompanied by my friend Kimly and his friend Sambath, a tall country boy visiting Wat Phnom for the first time. These two smiled good naturedly at the twitching, tattooed youths clutching yellow-smeared plastic bags while I hurried ahead into the museum, worried about my safety.

There was no-one there to admit us. Indeed, the whole museum was empty of people. Empty, that is, apart from an entire family (with cats) who had set up house in a dark, distant corner of the ground floor near the back emergency exit. These guys were busy. They were cooking, hanging out laundry, doing all the things you would do if you lived on a campsite in a municipal museum. Kimly shouted to them. 'Just go in,' called out a woman who was squatting down over a plastic tub washing a saucepan. 'Someone will be there by the time you leave—you can pay them then.'

The ground floor looked like a total write-off. Apart from the family, a whole half of it was given over to a display of terrible art for sale to tourists. 'Nothing to see down here,' offered our helpful housewife. 'Go straight upstairs.'

Now, someone had once obviously held great hopes for this museum. It was a part of an ongoing transformation of the Wat Phnom area into a respectable and modern park. Tethered elephants and feral monkeys, solicitors, pimps and dealers of every description had all been removed to create this museum, which had obviously promptly fallen into complete neglect, slowly ceding its territory back to the squatters and miscreants who had always claimed this space as their own.

Upstairs was a series of dimly lit dioramas showing the various epochs and triumphs of the Khmer people. When we came to the scene of the construction of Angkor Wat, Sambath turned to me solemnly and said, 'Notice how big and strong the men in this scene are. Nothing at all like the puny Khmer around today. We were once a race of giants, you see.'

'Really?' I said.

'Oh yes,' he assured me, his face taking on a mysterious mien. 'Haven't you stopped to think how extraordinary Angkor Wat actually is? It could never have been constructed by normal men, giants or not. No, there is magic involved—all Cambodians know this. The Khmer were once masters of magic, and our nation was great. All gone now . . .' This is actually a reasonably commonly held belief. Cambodian authors Vichean Khun and Chenthy He point out that it was once thought that the temples had been designed and built by the god Vishnu himself.

Kimly ambled over and, tapping at the glass, he pointed to one of the small papier-mâché figures and started to giggle. 'Look,' he said, 'you can see her boobs.'

We went through a small section devoted to traditional Khmer dance. 'Cambodian dancing, very beautiful,' said Sambath. 'Stolen, of course, by the Thai.' A little further on was a depiction of Khmer boxing, a drawing of extravagantly muscled, almost-naked men locked in violent embraces. 'Cambodian boxing,' intoned Kimly. 'Very good, best in the world. Stolen by the Thai. We must fix this situation. Thai boxing! There is no such thing.'

By now the mood of my two friends was quite sombre. We came upon a new display, a huge, pixellated but proudly spotlighted blow-up of Preah Vihear, the ancient ruined temple on the Thai–Cambodian border that had been the site of significant military tension between the two countries, each claiming ownership and each willing to trade shots and the occasional death of a poor young soldier in its defence.

We stood before it. The ruined temple was a symbol that was becoming increasingly popular in Cambodia, this very image popping up in restaurants and cheap hotel lobbies, a visual statement of ownership. Of course, no-one had actually been to Preah Vihear, as it was difficult and expensive to reach from the Cambodian side. I looked at the faces of Kimly and Sambath and both were angry and scornful. They spoke to each other animatedly in Khmer, occasionally translating a snatch of their denunciation for me. 'The Thai won't be happy till Cambodia is their colony . . . we must do everything to keep our territory . . . the arrogance and violence of that race . . . the Thai can claim nothing as their own, their entire civilisation was stolen from the Khmer . . .'

Until now I had only been privy to the obsessive hatred the Khmer felt for the Vietnamese. This new ancient grudge took me by surprise, though I had read about it and was well aware of the Preah Vihear conflict. I was to come across it more and more, however. People were afraid to travel to Thailand, and warned their friends against it. Those who had been to the border reported on the arrogance and unfriendliness of the Thais they encountered there. Once I said that a friend in Battambang looked Thai and he had become angry and offended. 'Never say that to a Khmer person,' he said. 'It is a great insult.' I was quick to learn never to underestimate the ancestral hatreds and feuds of the Khmer. They are a tenacious but put-upon race, having struggled for territory against their neighbours for millennia.

When we came downstairs a plump woman was sitting at the front counter getting her toenails cut by one of the Vietnamese women who wander the park with large boxes full of the pedicurist's tools of trade. As we paid belatedly for our entry, she asked us how we'd enjoyed the museum.

'Excellent,' said Kimly. 'A fine display. Makes me proud to be Khmer.'

MONKS AND EXCELLENCIES

The Tonlé Sap lake lies at the heart of Cambodia. The largest freshwater lake in South-East Asia, it begins at

Angkor and transforms itself into a river that flows all the way to Phnom Penh, a perfect journey from the ancient into the modern. And once in Phnom Penh it becomes suitably fractious and unpredictable. The river does something frankly magical once a year: it reverses its flow. The Khmer people were so impressed by this feat they accord it mystical significance, and the season of its happening remains one of the most important holidays on the Cambodian calendar.

I refuse to understand how it actually happens. Of course, there is a perfectly adequate scientific explanation, but I am uninterested in it, no matter how often and how carefully it is explained to me. It remains a true wonder, something so bizarre that any rational explanation is surplus to its needs. Right in the middle of the capital city of Cambodia a vast river decides to temporarily flow backwards every year.

Boat trips are, for me, a great treat, and when I discovered that you could travel up this river and across the Tonlé Sap lake to Siem Reap, the modern day city that sits next to the ruins of Angkor, I booked a ticket. The woman at the travel agency on the river was small and beautifully dressed, her hair sprayed into a helmet of perfection. 'What do you do, sir?' she asked.

'Well, at the moment I am a travel writer.'

'Sir! Let me give you my card. Please recommend my travel service. There is so much you can do to help Cambodia.'

This unusual request didn't really faze me, as total strangers requesting favours are reasonably common-place in Cambodia. Many foreign visitors are in fact there for humanitarian reasons, and English-speaking Cambodians in the tourist sector are perfectly aware that appealing to this crusading side of the Western psyche is likely to butter people up.

I asked the woman how long the boat trip might be and she looked confident and told me, 'Five hours—at the most.' Naturally it came closer to seven.

But it was so lovely drifting up that river on its brown waters and looking directly in to Vietnamese fishing villages—the fishermen seem always to be Vietnamese—and farms that roll down to the water. This is Cambodia at its most bucolic. It is the landscape that people fall in love with, flat and gentle and largely unpopulated, a hot, tropical idyll that seems almost perfect. And looking out on it, it is almost impossible to imagine the horrors that were performed on these very fields. People are inclined to fall in love with Cambodia because they come expecting a scene of war-torn misery and discover instead a sleepy, slow-moving little country where people smile and laugh and attempt to get on with their lives. It comes as a surprise to the tourist who has come seeking horror and, it must be said, a relief.

But travel is a distant dream to most Cambodians. While almost everyone has been to Siem Reap to see Angkor Wat and to a distant province to see their ancestral land, few can make any claim to a wider experience of tourism. A few people I met told similar tales of having travelled to another province in order to visit a shaman, magician or healer during a family health crisis, and many had parents who had lived in refugee camps in Thailand for a period, but beyond that there were very few holidays to be reported.

My own journeys were thus a source of intense interest on the part of my Cambodian friends. They could listen for hours to the trivial details of international travel, and loved nothing more than having me list the countries I'd visited, the cities I'd seen. 'And tell me, brother, how are the people there?' they would prompt me. 'The food? Are their cities civilised places? Skyscrapers? Trains?' When they discovered that I needed to make monthly trips outside of Cambodia in order to have my visa renewed, their eyes bulged. 'Impossible to imagine your wealth,' they would say.

My friend Panit had recently published a book of short stories about poor Cambodian farm boys lost in the big city of Phnom Penh. It is a common motif in Cambodian literature, as in Cambodian life. He was particularly fascinated by the process of travel and how it all worked. He insisted on accompanying me when I went to buy my air ticket to Ho Chi Minh City, but was hugely disappointed by the prosaic nature of what ensued. 'No different from buying a bus ticket,' he complained, glancing with contempt at the printed-out e-ticket. 'Why, I could make this up myself—what's stopping me from copying it and getting on any plane I wanted?'

While we were at the travel agent a huge 4WD pulled up right outside the front door, blocking all other access. A small, middle-aged Cambodian man in a white short-sleeved shirt got out, followed by two burly security guards. As soon as they entered the office the entire place was abuzz. I was completely ignored as each and every person there attended to this man's needs. Panit's eyes flashed with pleasure at the arrival, and at the knowledge that he was frequenting the same place as so elevated a personage. 'Who is it?' I asked, expecting it to be a prince or a government minister.

'I have no idea,' whispered Panit. 'But it is an Excellency! Very high status—you chose a good travel agent.'

The Cambodians run after perceived VIPs and treat them slavishly. These illustrious unknowns, marked out by their 4WDs, their bodyguards and their obscenely high-handed behaviour, are referred to universally in English as 'Excellencies'. Their photographs grace restaurant walls and hotel lobbies—in fact they frequently own those restaurants and hotels. No-one ever knows their names or what they do; it is enough that they are visibly rich and willing to insist on their status. Anyone prepared to block traffic with an expensive car and act like a wilful arsehole is eligible for the title of Excellency, though I believe there is a more formal system of honours in place.

Monks, too, hold elevated positions in Cambodian culture. Not so much the everyday monks, those too-familiar brothers, cousins and uncles who have entered the monastery for a short period to fulfil their duty to their mothers. But the more senior monastics, the elderly and very stern heads of big city monasteries, are just one step removed from royalty, and indeed can even command the respect of royalty. The abbott of Wat Botum, the largest monastery in the country, was one of these holy men. Quite elderly and infirm, in the evenings he could be seen by all taking his exercise—the briefest of walks across a temple courtyard—surrounded by young acolytes who held him up and matched his pace, shuffle for shuffle. Though sickly, he was still opinionated, and had stirred up quite a fuss by asking the authorities to ban the display of rotisserie meats outside restaurants. A roasting calf's carcass used to tempt diners was not, he felt, becoming to an avowedly Buddhist nation.

Panit had recently lost his mobile phone. It had been stolen from his bag while he was attending a concert in the foyer of the Sorya shopping mall. While he mourned the loss of an expensive phone, his greater sadness was the fact that it had included the personal numbers of several Excellencies, now all lost to him. I asked him if he'd ever called any of these powerful people, and he looked at me surprised and said, 'No!

77

I could never dare.' Nonetheless, the numbers represented a potential opportunity, and as such were valuable. I didn't ask how he'd come by them.

The phone had been so easily stolen because he'd foolishly left it in the open side-pocket of his backpack. 'Why on earth did you keep it in such a place?' I asked. 'Why wasn't it in your pocket?'

'In my pocket!' he said, aghast. 'Are you crazy? If I keep my phone in my pocket I will become sterile and never give my mother grandchildren. This is a fact. I heard it on Voice of America.' This was the trump card. Anything anyone heard on the Voice of America Khmer broadcast was taken as gospel.

Later we walked back to the riverside. It was, as usual, a hot day, and the early afternoon was quite unbearable. I begged to be allowed to spend an hour or so at a ritzy air-conditioned cafe. Panit was more than happy to do this, because it meant that we would be surrounded by Western tourists and expats, every movement and utterance of whom fascinated him.

At the table near us sat a young foreign man dressed carefully in tie and shirt sleeves, attended by his Khmer translator. A set of plans or legal documents were spread out on the table in front of them, and the foreign man was clearly frustrated by something. 'There's always exceptions!' he said. 'Always someone who's allowed to do something differently, to change the guidelines. We can't work like this! Why can't everyone just stick to the rules?'

I smiled to myself and imagined the horror of doing business in Cambodia. I felt his aggravation.

TUOL SLENG GENOCIDE MUSEUM

I think it's Tuol Sleng that brings the full weight of Cambodia's horrific past down on the tourist. It's because of its mundane architecture, its recognisable utility. It's the kind of place that should only ever have been a school. When I first visited in the mid-90s it was still overgrown, ramshackle. Families lived on site and, glancing out of the window of a torture chamber, I could see young men playing volleyball and women cooking. In many ways it was even more emotionally wrenching. How on earth could they live at this place of so many ghosts?

But now it is tidied and slickly operated. You can buy overpriced souvenirs, including replica Khmer Rouge outfits. I'm not quite sure what kind of person would buy a Khmer Rouge costume having just seen the extent of their murderous evil, but there's obviously some kind of demand. I took my parents there and we dutifully lined up to buy a book and have it signed by

Bou Meng, the onsite survivor, who must surely be one of Cambodia's richest and hardest-working authors. While I was in Cambodia, one of the English-language newspapers ran a story about him, and he was proud that he had bought two houses with the proceeds from his memoir of torture, loss and miraculous salvation. He said he would sit there signing books till the day he died.

It is a small book, painful to read, dedicated to his wife, the young and beautiful Ma Yoeun, who was tortured and murdered at the prison. Her photograph is there in the front of the book, one of the photographs taken of each prisoner at Tuol Sleng before their torture began. Comrade Duch, the prison's overseer, had a mania for documenting the people he saw and the things he ordered. Survivor Bou Meng says in the book that sometimes, looking at her picture, he can think of nothing but how horrible her final days must have been. I'm not sure why I lined up to see this sad, shrunken little man as he sat at a rickety wooden desk in a shed on the Tuol Sleng grounds. Was he a strange kind of celebrity? He barely looked up at me as he signed the book. He didn't smile. Some people wanted photographs with him, and he stared up at the camera with that same guarded face. His terrible misfortune had become his job.

His biography is less than clear. He was himself a part of the Khmer Rouge movement, an ideologue who, along with his beloved wife, fled into the jungles of Cambodia to join the guerrilla resistance and to paint pictures of Marx and Lenin for his comrades. And then, like so many in the vicious and paranoid Khmer Rouge infrastructure, his fortunes changed and he turned from victor to victim, his entire family sent to Tuol Sleng for unknown crimes against the Party. Bou Meng's murky and complicated involvement with the regime he now despises echoes the experience of so many Cambodians. As I was to discover time and time again, so many people in modern day Cambodia had some degree of involvement in, and compliance with, the Khmer Rouge.

On certain days of the week young women in business suits from the Documentation Center of Cambodia come along to the Tuol Sleng museum to give a talk about what exactly had happened there. These sleekly groomed and beautiful girls have doctorates from English universities and must surely be as bewildered by the site as we all are. Not many people come to these 'classes'. The day we were there the classroom had no electricity so the fans couldn't be turned on and we all began to sweat in the monstrous heat. An unruly group of Cambodian senior high school boys were herded in, heightening the heat, stuffiness and sweaty smell of the room. They were shy and silent when faced by these impossibly polished and beautiful women in front of them, barely older than they.

Zoning out from the monotone lecture being delivered by the women, I began to read the graffiti etched onto the desk in front of me. Someone—probably a member of another high school group—had scratched in the names of all the members of Teen Top, the Korean boy band of the moment. Next to each name was a rating system of hearts. I wondered if I should add my own opinion, but the school boys had begun to ask a series of painful questions in English, and so I stood up and stumbled out of the room, dazed by the heat.

From the verandah of this third-floor school building, a place where men, women and children had been imprisoned, bound, tortured, beaten and killed, I could see the emerging prosperity of the district surrounding it. There were several tall, new hotels, and at least two day spas whose signs I could read. There were groovy little cafes and interesting restaurants in the adjacent streets. All of this had come about because Tuol Sleng was one of the country's premier tourist attractions. The customary Cambodian concern about ghosts and spirits seems to have been bypassed here.

I wandered through the exhibitions absently. I had been so many times before that its impact on me was negligible, though I still became emotional in the rooms full of photographs of the prison's victims. These tormented eyes and barely contained grimaces were too raw and real to ever be ignored. And I always looked at them for faces I might recognise, and I seemed to recognise them all. Handsome jaws, high cheekbones, sleek, dark skin and black, glinting eyes. These were faces I knew from outside, beautiful, desirable faces. Except these were really the faces of the dead, people destined to be electrocuted, beaten with iron bars, mutilated and torn apart, the whole process carefully recorded in manila folders in the evil bureaucracy of death maintained by the Khmer Rouge.

In one room is an exhibition of the trials and deaths of various Khmer Rouge figures. There was a large photograph of Comrade Duch, the Khmer Rouge's principal torturer and the head of the Tuol Sleng prison. People had vandalised the image, writing things in Khmer in white-out pen. His eyes had been pushed out by pens and pencils, over and over again. Duch was the last remaining Khmer Rouge identity of any seniority, and had become the focal point of everyone's anger about the past. Films were made about him, he was constantly in the newspaper. A clever, softly spoken man, he had converted to Christianity and had for many years worked under an alias for a charity organisation. He had repented fully, he said, though no-one seemed to believe him.

Foreign politicians come now to Tuol Sleng, hurried through this horrific series of rooms in order to make who knows what point. While I was there the Australian foreign minister came. He pledged 1.6 million dollars to the ill-fated tribunal to seek justice for the pointless genocide perpetrated by the Khmer Rouge. This tribunal was the talk of the town, filling up the English-language newspapers and the Khmer-language TV channels. But

I couldn't help but wonder about all this money spent on revenge in a country with few hospitals and no effective postal system. Not for the first time I wondered if Cambodia wasn't being forced into a backward-focus by the cashed up foreign donors and keenly empathising tourists.

A few nights later my parents, who had come to Cambodia to visit me, took me to the Bophana Centre, a non-profit organisation dedicated to preserving the audio-visual culture of Cambodia. In their tiny screening room they were showing a stark and unnerving documentary about Comrade Duch made by French-Khmer director Rithy Panh. It is a long, rambling, meditative one-on-one interview with the torturer, who alternately begs forgiveness and attempts to excuse his own actions. Duch's take is that he was a mere cog in the Khmer Rouge machinery, a man carrying out orders, a victim himself.

THE BUDDHA'S EYEBROW

Right on Sisowath Quay, in perhaps the coolest and breeziest spot in all of Phnom Penh, sits Wat Ounalom, a temple devoted to a relic of the Buddha's eyebrow.

This prosaic relic is no odder than the multitudinous relics that populate the Christian world, and certainly a great deal more elevating than, for example, Christ's foreskin. Nonetheless, it managed to raise a giggle from Trong, a friend visiting from Saigon, when I explained to him what it was. We had come to be blessed and to have a sacred red thread tied around our wrists. Trong, convinced of the magical superiority of the Khmer, had seen hundreds of people wandering around Phnom Penh with these threads, and had determined that that was exactly the kind of thing he needed to have before he returned home.

Trong was a tall, pale-skinned hairdresser from downtown Ho Chi Minh City. We were old friends, and as soon as he discovered I was in Phnom Penh he jumped on a bus and took the five-hour trip to see me. While in Saigon he was an unremarkable—if slightly camp—presence; on the streets of Phnom Penh he was a figure of wonder. His tallness, paleness, beauty and effeminacy were all noteworthy, and everyone stared at him as he strode the streets in tight purple T-shirts and skinny jeans. Trong, however, seemed oblivious to the attention, and chattered away to me in loud Vietnamese, filling me in on all the latest Saigon gossip.

My quiet, reserved Cambodian friends were perplexed by him, and some of them took me aside and said earnestly, 'I fear that your Vietnamese friend might be a gay.' What was most surprising was that, despite never before having left Ho Chi Minh City, Trong seemed to have more friends in Phnom Penh than I did. People would run out of cafes and hairdressing salons to greet him, and at bars and nightclubs there would invariably be someone who would cry out, 'Trong! What on earth are you doing here?'

Like the Thais, the Vietnamese credit the Cambodians with having an edge when it comes to matters magical. Even Khmer writing on its own is viewed as possessing magical qualities, and written spells and charms will often contain pieces of Khmer script. This all takes on a somewhat racist quality in Vietnam proper, and in Saigon, Khmer people are sometimes viewed with fear and suspicion, credited as magicians and spell-casters and rumoured to be able to do all sorts of wicked things through supernatural means. When I would go to stay in Khmer areas in regional Vietnam my city friends would warn, 'Do be careful—they have potions which they put in their food to make you love them. And then if you leave them you will be afflicted with tumours and rashes. It's best not to go.'

But this was all part of the attraction for Trong, who had a deep interest in matters mystical and was a regular habitué of seances and psychics in Saigon. From the moment he arrived in Phnom Penh we were on an exhausting whirl of temple and shrine visits, searching for luck, blessing and, hopefully, a magical edge in matters worldly. When we began to ask around about the red threads we were told by several people that the luckiest ones were to be had at Wat Ounalom.

Like most temples in the city, the business end of Wat Ounalom, its shrine, prayer and meditation halls, was the mere tip of the iceberg. Behind it, for two city blocks, was the real heart of the monastery, a hodgepodge collection of houses and dormitories filled with monks, young students from the country and scores of men of all ages who simply couldn't afford to live anywhere else—city temples are de facto homeless men's shelters. There is also normally a rambling cemetery containing the memorials to dead monks and rich lay people.

When Trong and I stumbled into the cemetery, a wild-haired woman ran up to us from behind one of the monuments. 'Sirs!' she cried. 'Come with me—you are very lucky.' Trong pinched me with delight as she led us to the largest and most elaborate monument, pulling out an enormous key to unlock its ornate doors. Inside sat a tiny old man, blinking and blind, in front of a small shrine. 'Lucky man!' she said as we ducked down and squeezed into the room. The man began to mumble to us in French, and Trong responded helpfully in Vietnamese, 'We don't understand you, old grandfather.'

The old man and the woman conferred in Khmer, and the only word I could distinguish was *Youn*, the derogatory Cambodian word for 'Vietnamese person'. Trong smiled on in blissful ignorance and finally the wild-haired woman said, 'Lucky man!' and pointed again to the little old blind man locked in the tomb. I had the feeling she had exhausted her English vocabulary. Trong gestured to his wrist, wrapping two long and elegantly manicured fingers around it in imitation of a bracelet. The woman shrieked in relief, and, reaching behind the shrine, she pulled out an elaborate metal tray piled high with red threads cut in lengths.

Holding our hands in prayer position, we kneeled in front of the old man as he began to chant in Pali, the sacred language of Theravada Buddhism. The woman tied the bright red threads around Trong's wrist, and then turned to mine. The easy job suddenly became difficult, as it became apparent that my chubby wrist was almost double the girth of Trong's beautifully slender one. The threads only just made it around, leaving very little room indeed for the elaborate knot she had tied before. Somehow she managed it, but while Trong's sacred threads floated loosely around his wrist, mine were pulled tight, cutting into the flesh. Trong's may have been stylishly magical, but mine had the beginnings of a tourniquet, and I feared that if we didn't get out soon I might lose circulation to my hand.

The ceremony over, another raised tray was produced, this one covered in a white cloth and a single five dollar bill, a helpful guide as to the 'contribution' expected. Trong blissfully slapped a single dollar down on the tray and began to shuffle backwards out of the tiny, stifling space. The woman was aghast and said something to the old man, who responded in a gruff stream from which, once more, floated that nasty word *Youn*. I managed to cough up the requisite five dollars. The woman looked doubtfully at it and gestured to Trong outside, holding up two fingers in a way that told me she was expecting five dollars *each*. She brightened up when I pulled out a ten, though her smile faltered for a moment when I snatched the five dollar bill off the tray to make my own change. Still, things became much more amicable and the old man showered us with blessings.

Once outside in the blinding sun, Trong almost skipped with pleasure at our new acquisitions. 'Oh, the luck!' he cried. 'They will be so jealous in Saigon. This is just perfect.' He held up his wrist and shook the red threads, moving them up and down with ease. My own hand was starting to hurt. Once we got back home I said I needed to shower and, sneaking a pair of scissors into the bathroom, I snipped through the red threads. There was a deep welt in my wrist where the threads had been solidly embedded in my flesh. The palm of my hand had turned a funny, purplish colour.

It wasn't till a few days later that Trong noticed my bare wrist. 'Your thread! Where has it gone?'

'Fell off in the shower,' I lied nonchalantly.

'What bad luck,' he said, with genuine sorrow.

WALTER MASON

Loven Ramos was opening up a new gallery, shop and restaurant in Phnom Penh called ARTillery and so I invited Panit to accompany me to the opening. Tall, dark and very handsome, Panit was the perfect companion for such an evening, lifting my glamour quotient by a factor of six. The gallery was in an alleyway off Street 240. Actually, it was down several twisting alleys off Street 240, and as we branched down each one, Panit would say, 'Are you sure, brother? Surely not further?' But finally we bottomed out and ARTillery sat there looking splendid, equal parts Greek villa and ghetto fabulousness.

Loven is an entrepreneurial genius and a brilliant self-promoter. Part of an unlikely army of Filipinos who have come to Cambodia because they recognise an opportunity, he has established hotels, galleries, boutiques and restaurants across Cambodia, all of them trademarked with his arty cool. He was working the room and introduced me to his business partner Emma, who turned out to work for the NGO Friends International.

The opening night party at ARTillery was exactly what I expected—fun, trendy and very white. There was a smattering of Filipinos and exactly four Khmer people. I know because Panit counted them all gleefully. For a people obsessed with nationalist spirit, Cambodians are surprisingly delighted when they go to an event or place where they are in the minority. Of course, I recognised the reaction because I share it myself. This is the snobbery of the traveller, the horror of seeing your own kind at a place you have reached with great difficulty.

Panit basked in being the centre of exotic interest in the middle of his own country, and carefully avoided the eye of the other Cambodians. A young Australian woman was singing, but I was distracted by the expensive gift shop selling artisanal products and local couture. I was taken by the re-invented *krama*, a traditional khmer scarf, cut in half and screen printed with chinese dragons, a wonderful pan-Asian melange. I bought bundles, and Panit ran up to me with a glass of red saying, 'Grape wine—very delicious and very strong. Let's finish and have another!'

I am never very good at these events. I inevitably end up shy, bored and headachey, and I pounce upon people who are brave enough to talk to me, grateful at last to not look like a complete reject. Of course, the danger in this is being landed in the company of the other party bore, and this is almost inevitably what happens. The insecure will always drift into each other's company.

A man standing next to me introduced himself. In late middle age, he said he was a journalist from Canada, in Cambodia to visit friends. 'You have to meet my wife,' he said, and so I agreed. We walked across the courtyard to where a white-haired woman dressed in a studiedly bohemian fashion was holding court to a group of younger people. 'Darling,' said the Canadian, tapping the woman on the shoulder. 'You must meet Walter, a writer from Australia.'

Turning slightly to look at me, she scowled and said, 'Another writer, how dull,' and then she turned back to her group. The Canadian and I were both rather taken aback. I don't think I had ever been so elaborately snubbed in all my life. The Canadian giggled and said, 'Oh, she's quite a character. She puts up with a lot from me, you know.' Somehow I doubted it, but I nodded graciously and moved on.

I soon met up with another man of almost exactly the same type. This one admitted to being in Cambodia for absolutely no reason at all—he was, in fact, looking for a reason. Panit joined us, holding high his glass of wine, his face flushed from enjoyment. Then something extraordinary happened. I introduced him to the lost man, and this fellow, looking Panit up and down, said to me, 'When are you leaving Cambodia?'

'Oh, in a few months,' I replied.

'Well, when you leave, would you mind if I called your friend?'

Panit and I both stood there blinking. We were completely stunned by the old seducer's effrontery. 'I rather think that's up to him,' I stumbled, my insane impulse of courtesy stopping me from being rude.

'Absolutely not!' said Panit, cheerfully, turning away to hunt down another glass of red.

There is a strange sort of reverse snobbery at work in expatriate establishments in Cambodia, which forbids the use of air-conditioning. Coming from Thailand or Vietnam, where most places are chilled to arctic levels (you actually need a jacket in the 7-Elevens of Bangkok), it comes as quite a shock. The groovier and more foreigner focused the place is in Cambodia, the less likely it is to be air-conditioned. It was no different at ARTillery, and I became so hot (the fans were pointless, blowing hot air upon the assembled) and thirsty that I hunted down Panit and together we walked up Street 240 to the Firefly Bar where I drank Coke after Coke and ate spaghetti. Panit chose a very expensive steak, which he ate with obvious relish.

Panit's eyes flashed with pleasure. He loved the bar. 'American style—I like! I think it's high class!' I asked how his steak was and he said, delightedly, 'Bland—very bland.' Down to about the last third of his meal, he pushed it aside.

'You're not going to finish that?' I asked, worried he mightn't like it, and also smarting at the knowledge of how much it cost.

'Oh no,' he said. 'I dare not eat all of the food on my plate, no matter how delicious. It makes me look greedy. If these waitresses saw me eat it all they would mock me as a country boy. They would smirk.'

SCHEDULED AMBITION

My cafe friend Kimly was always telling me he was 'scheduled' to do things I was almost certain would never happen. It's not that he is a fantasist, more that he has high and constantly shifting hopes, and the things he desires he is able to imagine into a kind of certainty.

'I am scheduled to visit Australia in the next few months,' he said to me once. 'How much would it cost me, approximately, for food, guest house and transport for two months?' How do I even answer such a question? Apart from having no idea what it might cost a young Cambodian man to support himself in Sydney for two months (an unimaginable amount, I am almost certain), how do I tell him that there is no chance in hell my nation would ever even grant him a visa to make that mythical visit? I am consumed with shame when confronted with this. I have travelled freely to his country, and been given permission to stay there for some time with nary a question as to my background and income. Should the tables be turned, he would be interrogated, shamed, made to jump all kinds of nearly impossible bureaucratic hurdles and then almost certainly refused entry at the end of it. How is this even fair, in our 'globalised' world? How can

I explain this to my eager young friend without exposing the fundamental inequality at the heart of our worlds?

So instead I lied, and said, 'Oh, maybe two or three thousand?'

He couldn't hide the disappointment on his face. 'As much as that?' he said, quite unbelieving. After a moment he asked, 'What would it cost me in Ho Chi Minh City?' opting for an altogether more realistic goal.

Kimly's shoes are a disgrace. They are cheap Chinese loafers, an essential part of his shabby 'professional' look. He is proud to be always dressed in trousers and a button shirt and shoes, and casual wear is completely banned in his world. Every time he comes to see me he is dressed as though for a business conference, even clutching a sheaf of papers and a tatty manila folder.

'Have you been to a meeting?' I asked.

'Going to one, with you,' he replied. And often our encounters took on the vibration of a meeting, with Kimly peppering me with questions about the world outside Cambodia, and occasionally even offering me frankly awful business opportunities. The strange thing was, I never really felt exploited or abused by our relationship. I knew that I was the measure of Kimly's upward mobility, and something thrilled me about his desperate ambition.

For all his bravado, Kimly, a young man who had grown up in an orphanage in Kampong Speu, a few hours out of Phnom Penh, had a ghastly job, and I admired the spin he managed to put on it, re-casting it as one of the endless 'opportunities' he saw the world possessing. He worked for a low-grade advertising agency, and his job consisted of doing all of the most embarrassing and menial things they could throw at him. So he woke early to hand out flyers about cheap English classes at traffic intersections. Then for the rest of the day he would scoot about Phnom Penh on a borrowed moped picking up and delivering printing jobs. Then in the afternoon he would stand outside rival English colleges and hand out leaflets to the students as they left, offering them cheaper classes. For this last job he was frequently yelled at and threatened, and once even beaten.

Kimly is a small man, slender and fine boned, and the thought of security guards beating him always strikes me as particularly cruel. But Kimly's tenacity was great, and he simply shook his head in a world-weary way and said, 'Part of the job, Walter, part of the job.' After leaving his orphanage, Kimly seemed to have possessed an innate talent to find himself awful positions. Almost his first paid job was on a Chinese fishing vessel which took him to sea for four years. The workers were paid on a sliding scale according to nationality, Cambodians at the bottom and Filipinos on top, because they could speak English. Eventually the owner of the ship dumped him in Hong Kong, telling him he didn't need any papers. Turned out the fellow was lying, and poor Kimly found himself in prison for some months before he was deported back to Cambodia, the end of a glorious career. 'Not a good man, Walter,' he said about his previous employer with delicious understatement. 'But at least I saw the world.'

He took great pride in his hair, which could change radically from one day to the next. Hairdressing seemed an unlikely preoccupation for such an overtly masculine man, but Kimly was much influenced by the Korean singers fawned over by Cambodian girls everywhere, and he thought his chances with the ladies might improve if he could persuade his thick, black hair into a style more imitative of these heart throbs. 'A guardian angel lives on the heads of all Cambodians,' he said to me, running his hand through today's not-quite-successful style. 'That is why we do not touch each other's heads. A girl, especially, cannot touch the head of a man. This would be a very bad thing.' The only exception to this was mothers, who had the sole right to touch their sons' heads with impunity. Indeed, this was a symbolic and deeply significant act. For a son to lay his head in his mother's lap and have his hair stroked was something supremely beautiful, and the ultimate act of sacrifice. Angels, said Kimly, were never bothered by a mother's touch; they were soothed by it.

One day, Kimly told me that the Cambodian government was scheduled to clear all beggars from Phnom Penh in the next year or so. He despises beggars. Once, while we were walking down Street 240, I was confronted by a beggar who possessed a truly upsetting collection of disabilities: his body was tiny and he had no legs, pushing himself around on a skateboard with the one arm he had. But his head was enormous, his facial features misshapen—lips twisted, eyes askew. He asked me for money but, seeing Kimly, he grunted and began to push himself away. I chased after the man and handed him a few dollars. Running back to Kimly, we walked along in silence until he turned to me and said, 'You shouldn't have given that man any money.'

'But why on earth not?' I asked. 'Look at the poor fellow. He's one of the ones who seems to have a good reason to beg.'

'Didn't you see the way he tried to avoid us once he saw me? We live together at the pagoda. Walter, he is the richest man in the place! Every day tourists give him fifty, sixty dollars. People hand him ten dollar bills. He has an iPhone! You know what I'd give to have an iPhone?' I giggled at the news, pleased by the fellow's good fortune. 'Don't laugh,' said Kimly with great seriousness. 'The man brings shame to the city. He drinks and has a girlfriend.'

'But look at him,' I said. 'There is nothing else he could possibly do in this country. How else could he get money?'

Shaking his head, Kimly muttered, 'He is a rich and shameful man. I will be glad when they clear the beggars from Phnom Penh.'

It took me a long time to realise that Kimly was one of the most notorious and respected street hustlers in my area. His swaggering, fast walk was something I noticed other young toughs affected. He knew each and every tuk tuk driver, most of whom were single men who, like him, lived in lean-tos and corridors in the endless dormitories of Wat Botum. The wat was a clearing house for reprobates and layabouts. Kimly wanted to transcend his past—he was trying desperately, but his own bad habits constantly came back to claim him.

One day he had borrowed a motorcycle—at least, I hope he had borrowed the motorcycle—and wanted to drive me to a distant temple famous for its statuary. When we finally reached it he dropped me at the gates and told me he was going to find a place to safely park the motorcycle. The temple seemed to have fallen on hard times, as it was largely deserted and the statues were mostly crumbling, the paint peeling, the concrete cancerous. There were several large religious buildings whose construction had been begun but at some obviously distant point abandoned, and so they sat about, vast, dangerous ruins.

The ugliness and decrepitude of the complex was actually quite enchanting, and a photographer's dream. In the middle of the temple's graveyard was a small wooden shack of great age and beauty, dusty and dissolving in the humidity, surrounded by a number of huge statues of Buddha and Vishnu, the Earth Goddess, monks, saints and mythical creatures. It looked like they had all been brought here for repair, as each had a fatal fault, if not many. Heads lolled or were missing altogether, arms were absent, with only a profusion of cables sticking out from cement sockets. I was photographing this bizarre statue graveyard like crazy when, with unnerving slowness, one of the wooden shutters of the shack was pulled open from inside and an ancient monk scowled out at me. He shouted at me in Khmer, and, utterly spooked, I ran back out into the heat and destruction of the main temple complex.

I found Kimly leaning rakishly on his elbows against an allegorical figure representing sickness and suffering. 'Pretty amazing, huh?' he said, gesturing to the tortured face of the statue. 'Take a picture of me here.' And at that he assumed a tough guy pose, as he did at each of the consecutive statues, occasionally throwing hip-hop-style gang signs, or crossing his arms haughtily like a pimp rapper. It didn't seem to me an attitude to be taking at a place of worship, no matter how decrepit it might be. We sidled up to a huge artificial pond, half full and stagnant, covered with a rank algae. 'Boy, this place has really gone downhill,' said Kimly, turning to me with an apologetic smile. As he did I was nearly knocked over by the smell of alcohol coming from his breath.

'Did you have a drink?' I asked him, worried because we had a long drive home.

Kimly opened his eyes wide for a moment, obviously considering the option of lying, until he finally said, 'Yes, brother. But just one tiny glass of wine. The man who parked my motorcycle gave it to me.'

I discovered that he had chosen to park the motor-cycle at a filthy little wine shop, where a small group of men sat on small plastic chairs and drank themselves into the heat of the afternoon. They all cheered on seeing me, especially when I climbed up onto the motorcycle behind the diminutive Kimly. One of them came forth clutching two little glasses of clear rice wine, the home-made kind that had recently killed a number of people at a wedding party in the provinces. I had promised my father that I would not touch any home-made alcohol, but in this case it was a promise impossible to uphold. We threw down the strong wine and drove out onto the open road. I was instantly nauseous, the suspect alcohol disagreeing with my empty, thirsty stomach and the intense heat outside.

'Nice men,' shouted Kimly into the wind as we sped along the road. 'Very funny. They said you were fat, and that it would be impossible for me to drive you back to Phnom Penh.' I wrapped my arms tight around Kimly's slender waist, sick now and suddenly very scared. I felt a superstitious twinge at what the men had said.

PYONGYANG RESTAURANT

Cambodia has a peculiar friendship with North Korea. King Sihanouk had once written a poem celebrating the glory of the great dictator Kim Il Sung, who had in turn housed and protected the Cambodian royals during some of the tougher periods of Cambodian history. Cambodia is one of the only countries in the world where North Korea has any kind of diplomatic and official presence, and where you can actually meet North Koreans. They maintain a somewhat down-at-heel embassy in one of Phnom Penh's most visible locations, right next door to Prime Minister Hun Sen's palatial residence near the Independence Monument. I would make a point of walking by it on my nightly constitutionals, peering in at the gates and stopping to look at the enigmatic noticeboard featuring pictures of Kim Jong-Il's corpse. I longed for an invitation in, but mostly I was just chased away by a scowling young Cambodian soldier posted at the gate.

My friend Panit told me that there were North Korean students at his university, but that they weren't exactly the best mixers. 'Very unfriendly,' he said. 'And plain! You can't tell the boys from the girls, their haircuts and clothes are so similar. Not fashionable, Walter! Not at all.'

'Could you introduce me to some?' I asked, excited at the possibility.

'Not possible,' he said with conviction. 'They talk to nobody. Probably they are afraid to. They come in, they go out, they never speak to the Cambodians.'

The only other option was for me to visit the Pyongyang Restaurant, one of the world's only North Korean restaurants and something of a tourist attraction in its own right. I took my partner Thang with me. He was in Cambodia for a visit and, as a noted foodie and blogger, I thought this might be something that would amuse him. For me, committed Orientalist and exoticist that I am, it was purely the thrill of meeting North Koreans that drew me there.

When we arrived the large and plainly furnished restaurant was filled with large tables of drunken South Koreans, there for their own kind of thrill. The waitresses were all very young and very beautiful, with startlingly white skin, dressed in preposterous little-girl dresses made of luridly coloured polyester, all frills and flounces. There were large signs everywhere telling visitors not to take photographs, and Thang, in his inimitable fashion, pulled out his enormous digital SLR and began snapping away furiously at everything that caught his eye.

This brought the attention of our assigned waitress. She was by far the most beautiful of all the waitresses, but also the most savage in demeanour, and she bore down on us with a terrifying scowl. 'No photos, sir!' she said, pointing at the sign directly above Thang's head, only one of about a dozen within eyeshot.

'Oh gosh!' said Thang breezily. 'I hadn't realised.'

For some peculiar and very stupid reason I thought I might ease tension, and my own embarrassment, by saying, 'Oh, don't worry, he's just taking photos to put on his blog. You know, the internet.'

'The internet!' cried our waitress, her fierce eyes bulging. 'No! You must not.' I had forgotten that North Korea's leaders don't take such a rosy view of the internet. She then insisted on looking at every photograph Thang had taken in the restaurant, plus a good dozen or so before, just to be sure. This seemed to be the principal duty of all the waitresses, who were constantly bearing down on old Korean men snapping away on their mobile phones. Certainly their more traditional role, that of taking orders and serving food, was less scrupulously observed.

Almost as soon as our lacklustre—and moderately expensive—meal was served, the waitresses all took to the stage and served up a forty-minute all-singing, all-dancing variety show of dizzyingly camp value. While performing they all adopted a peculiar, and very creepy, childish voice and demeanour. They were all in their twenties, but on stage they sang in squeaky falsettos and mugged and minced like six-year-old beauty queens. This was obviously some kind of North Korean performance convention, but its artifice and weirdness unsettled me deeply. Not least because I knew that our waitress, who turned out to be the star turn, was a fearsome harridan and her sudden transformation into a black-haired Shirley Temple did not convince me for even a second.

There were folk dances, a drum solo, and a whole set of 'international' songs in English, Khmer and Chinese. It was our waitress who performed the Chinese song and, as soon as she was off stage and sweatily returned to her waitressing duties, I congratulated her in Mandarin and asked if she had studied the language. She looked up at me, startled, and demanded, 'Why do you speak Chinese?'

'Oh, it's just something I have studied,' I responded, shaken by her switch into interrogation mode.

A little later she was back at our table to refill our beers and she heard Thang and I speaking to each other in Vietnamese. 'You speak Vietnamese too?' she asked.

'Just a little,' I answered weakly, terrified now.

'What about Khmer?' she asked. 'Or . . . Korean?'

'No, no, none of those,' I assured her. For the rest of the meal she hung about us with undue attention. Floating by me, she would utter things softly to me in a variety of languages, seeing what response I gave.

'Oh God,' said Thang, 'she thinks you're a spy. I'll never get out of here with my camera now.' Soon after he'd been forbidden to use his camera, Thang had engaged in a kind of photographic subterfuge, pretending to send an extraordinary number of text messages as he held his phone high and oddly close to his eyes, all the while taking forbidden pictures of the entirely innocuous restaurant.

We became quite stressed by the end of the meal, not at all sure that we would get out of there with our personal property intact. I began to have a distinct feeling of what it might be like to live in North Korea. Our previously sullen waitress had transformed herself into a completely unbelievable pussycat, fixing me with terrifying, blank-eyed smiles. I was so spooked I left a ridiculously large tip, something I always do when I feel uncomfortable.

Just as we were about to walk out the door to freedom, a group of four waitresses came running towards us. Here it goes, I thought, we are about to be impounded. Lead by our own waitress, they shrieked and giggled. 'Are you living in Phnom Penh, big brother?' she asked me in Chinese.

'For a while, yes,' I said, almost instantly regretting my honesty.

'Well, can I have your number?' she asked. 'It is rare to meet such a smart man as you.'

Another of my failings is that I find it impossible not to give my phone number, no matter how clearly lunatic is the person asking for it. I smiled and wrote it down for her, with Thang glaring at me all the while. 'It's a honey trap!' he said as we walked down the dark driveway that lead from the restaurant. 'They're going to try to lure you back and then drug you and take you to Pyongyang and steal your organs or make you a brainwashed spy! Haven't you seen *The Manchurian Candidate*? The original one with Angela Lansbury, not that crap remake. It will be just like that.'

But, sadly, no-one ever called. I had visions of being smuggled down the Mekong River in a North Korean midget submarine, and then lead along a cold, grey beach into a military compound where I would learn to respond to stimuli and maybe get hired to make propaganda films. It looked like a rosy future. Whenever my phone rang with an unknown number I would grab it up and answer hurriedly, expectantly—was this going to be my big call? But invariably it was some monk I'd met in the countryside, or an unemployed actor I knew who had more than thirty SIM cards.

Desolate, I returned to the restaurant a few weeks later with some Cambodian friends. No-one recognised me at all, and this time we were assigned the dumpiest waitress who we saw exactly twice, once to take the order and once to deliver the entire meal. When the show started I attempted to make eye contact with my previous provocateur, but she glared right through me.

When we left, two sad and bored waitresses held the door open for us. 'What a terrific evening,' I said to them in Chinese, hoping to re-ignite their memory and restore my previous celebrity. They just looked at each other in a confused manner, bowed slightly and said, 'Thank you for coming,' in English before closing the door, softly and quietly, in my face.

CHOUENG EK KILLING FIELDS

Kimly had dropped by to see me, and I walked down to the hotel lobby to collect him. The way my guests were welcomed by my hotel was always an arbitrary process. Sometimes I would be showering or writing and a total stranger would knock at my door, having been blithely sent up by the people at the front desk. Then, on occasion, friends I saw every day and who were on first-name basis with all the hotel staff would be detained at the lobby and instructed to call me to come down and collect them. When I got downstairs, Kimly was sprawled on one of the hard wooden Chinese couches, chatting on the phone. Seeing me, he popped the phone in his shirt pocket and we began the slow and hot ascent back to my room on the top floor. We chatted the whole way, sharing a great many intimacies and discussing mutual friends in a scandalous manner.

Coming into my room, I heard a strange, metallic squawking issuing from Kimly's person. 'I think you forgot to hang up your phone,' I said pointing to his glowing top pocket.

'Oh no,' he responded. 'I'm still chatting with my friend at work.'

'How is that possible,' I asked, 'when you and I have been talking for at least the last ten minutes.'

'He doesn't mind,' said Kimly. 'He knows I am busy visiting my foreign friend.' At this Kimly fished out his phone and, flicking off his shoes, he sat down on one of my easy chairs and took up his conversation once more in earnest. I had noticed people's casual and intimate relationship with mobile telephony in Cambodia. It has an unregulated telecommunications market, so local calls can be remarkably cheap if you know which companies to use at which times. To maximise these economies, almost everyone I knew possessed a half-dozen SIM cards, which they would slip into their phones at different times of the day or when calling different people. This meant that I could never rely on caller ID, because people could often be using some long-neglected SIM card which had been sitting at the bottom of their bag for a month. 'Good rates this week,' they would explain, when I finally picked up the call. 'Cheap, cheap.'

Panit had a complex timetable of calls that necessitated leaving his phone open at the back so that he could swiftly transfer SIM cards as need presented. He was on a deal where, at a certain time each evening, he could call his father in Battambang completely free of charge for an hour. This meant that, no matter what he was doing, he would dial his father at the appointed time and simply stay on the line with him for the entire period. Frequently the phone would be left unattended on a bench, restaurant table or cinema seat, and a gruff, disembodied scream would mean his dad had something to say, at which point he would pick it up and hold it to his ear. Often, too, people had multiple conversations with friends and family members simultaneously on the several cheap phones that almost everyone had to house some of their SIM card collections. I was often on the receiving end of these immensely frustrating calls, and after a couple of minutes of neglect I would simply hang up. This, however, was seen as a perfectly acceptable social interaction—people rarely said goodbye when they hung up the phone.

One of the more disconcerting experiences of being in Phnom Penh is being trailed by a smiling tuk tuk driver once you go anywhere near one of the city's main tourist sites. 'Tuol Sleng Torture Museum, sir, Killing Fields, very nice, I will take you everywhere, cheap price . . .' Though it might be uncomfortable to confront, misery is business in Cambodia, and the horrific recent past has been recast as a truly unique tourist opportunity. I sit very uneasily with all of this, though like everyone else,

I have visited these places, and when people from other countries come to visit me in Cambodia they are among the first items on the sightseeing agenda.

It's hard to arrive at a clear moral position on the way genocide has been marketed in Cambodia. It is obviously important that the memory of such events be kept alive, and it even makes sense that sites of particular pathos, such as Tuol Sleng and the Killing Fields, be preserved as memorials to the memories of the millions who suffered and died. But the fact is, unlike at Angkor Wat, I very rarely saw Cambodians at these places. Despite a generation of education and intense government propaganda, most people I met under thirty had only the haziest idea of what actually went on during the Pol Pot regime. Indeed, people were more likely to invoke crazy anti-Vietnamese conspiracy theories than any actual historical facts, which always left me wondering how effective all of this memorialisation has been.

The normal 'afternoon of horror' is so much a part of the tourist route in Cambodia that, if you decide to visit the Killing Fields, the roads can get quite clogged with tuk tuks carrying their charges. After a genuinely affecting hour or so at Tuol Sleng, you take a longish tuk tuk ride out to Choueng Ek, the small village where the Khmer Rouge regime slaughtered and buried the prisoners they trucked out of Phnom Penh.

I had always resisted the urge to visit the Killing Fields. Just visiting Tuol Sleng made me feel ghoulish enough, and I questioned my own reasons for wanting to visit now. Was it merely an idle curiosity about mass murder? And if so, wouldn't it be better not to give in to such an unedifying interest? But Kimly was determined that I should have the full Cambodian tourism experience. I could never convince him that what I wanted to do was things that tourists normally never did. 'So you want to have a bad time? You want to be like a Cambodian and work all day in the sun? I can organise that for you, but don't expect me to come along.'

Kimly spent much of his time telling me about 'tourist places' of unimaginable fun and pleasure. These waterside restaurants, fun parks and points of scenic interest made up a list of places Kimly had heard about and always wanted to visit, and most of them sounded like places I would pay any money to avoid. Of course, finances were such that Kimly had never actually visited any of these places; they were merely spoken about by all of the other poor young men who slept on the floor of the pagoda buildings. Places once visited by parents, or seen during a school or orphanage trip, or the scene of a legendary family party in the distant past. None of the people Kimly knew had the leisure or money to visit these places, but they had become Edens in their imaginations.

'I have been planning for some time to visit the Killing Fields,' said Kimly in his gruff, serious voice. 'You must go there to understand Cambodia. So sad.

Many people died.' Of course, that represented the sum total of Kimly's knowledge of the Killing Fields, because he'd never been there. He engaged a tuk tuk, one of the drivers who also lived at the pagoda, a friend, he said, though he wasn't too sure of his name. Almost any good or service could be procured by Kimly from among his cohort at the pagoda. At various stages I had engaged the services of a barber, a translator, a tailor, an upholsterer and a bone-clicking masseur from the huge population of homeless men that lived in and around Wat Botum. Many of them had lived there for ten years or more, and saw no hope or chance of living anywhere else. They could rent you motorbikes, give you tattoos, buy you folk medicine and live poultry. It was a living, breathing mass of unexploited talent, and if anyone ever really wanted to transform Cambodia, all they would need to do is create an army from this huge population of the underemployed.

When we arrived at Choueng Ek the tuk tuk driver abandoned us at the gates and headed straight to the row of cheap cafes and restaurants that had sprung up to cater to waiting drivers. He was incredibly excited at the prospect, and left us in a cloud of dust. Kimly was both perplexed and thrilled by Choueng Ek. He was amazed by the audio tour headpieces handed out to visitors, but he quickly gave up on listening to the commentary and instead wandered, bored, around the site, the headphones hung about his neck. What he did do was get out one of his phones and dial up his friends and tell them about how he was touring the Killing Fields; the pleasure of the experience had to be mediated through the real-time retelling. Occasionally he would lift the headphones to his own phone's mouthpiece so that the person back in Phnom Penh could get a better sense of what was happening. He took seriously his duty of memorialisation, and we purchased incense and flowers and made our prostrations to the dead piled up in a modern *chedi*, a glass-sided reinvention of the traditional Buddhist memorial structure. Dusty skulls peered out at us from the glass as we circled them three times.

He cheered up noticeably when we went to the air-conditioned museum and cinema on the site. Staring around the exclusively international audience, Kimly said approvingly, 'All tourists! I am the only Khmer here. Good for my country.' Kimly set about accosting lone tourists, asking them their names, origins and plans for further travel. He always had about his person a stash of pamphlets and business cards for cheap hotels and buffet restaurants in Phnom Penh, and I doubt a single tourist visiting the Killing Fields that day came away without such a recommendation.

'This is a cool place,' he said, gesturing backwards over the fields that were the grave of thousands of his countrymen. 'I'd definitely come back.'

THE WONDERS OF SORYA

Across South-East Asia you often encounter the cult of the female soldier. In Vietnam they honour the *Hai Ba* Trung, sister-generals who slaughtered the Chinese invaders from the backs of elephants. In Korat in Thailand the central cult figure of the city is Thao Suranaree, a mayor's wife who got a heap of Laotian invaders drunk, thereby allowing their slaughter. In Cambodia travellers stop on the road to Siahnoukville to say a prayer at the cliffside shrine to Yiey Mao, a soldier's wife who trained as a warrior herself in order to avenge his death. The lovesick lady soldier is appeased by phallic offerings, and her roadside shrine has become a major institution because so many people fear for their lives on the dangerous road between Phnom Penh and Sihanoukville.

But the regular, twenty-first-century soldiers I saw on the streets of Phnom Penh were a distinctly less glamorous breed. Excessively plump, many of them seemed to have to provide some of their uniform themselves—particularly if they were higher up the chain of command. I would come across middle-aged soldiers in full combat fatigues accessorised with hideous cheap Chinese loafers with tassels.

The place to see these men in little teams of four or five was at Sorya shopping mall. Soldiers, high-society types, university students and scruffy Western backpackers were all much in evidence at Sorya, glorying in some of Phnom Penh's only properly functioning air-conditioning and strolling, half-crazed, among its stalls and tiny shops filled with things you'd almost certainly never want to buy. Sorya becomes a kind of desperate magnet for the bored of Phnom Penh, the inevitable spot to come to in moments of frustration. When life got too hard, or a place of rendezvous became too impossible to explain, I would inevitably say, 'Oh, let's just go to Sorya.'

One whole floor of Sorya is dedicated to the production and sale of pirated CDs, DVDs and games, and it is a film lover's paradise. I think I can, without censure or legal action, admit to buying the latest movies there and watching them on my laptop at my hotel. For the fact is, it is actually impossible to buy licensed entertainment products in Cambodia, unless they are locally produced. Anything foreign is available, in plenitude. All of the latest movies would be available at my favourite shop on the day of their cinematic release in America, if not a week or so before. The efficiency of the pirates' distribution was admirable, and I would urge any of the big entertainment groups in the West to recruit the best people in Cambodia and learn from their speed, thoroughness and attention to public demand. All I had to do was make a breezy enquiry about a movie and, if they didn't have it in stock, I would be accosted on the escalator a day or two later by a shop assistant saying, 'Sir, your movie is here.'

One day I was strolling restlessly through the floors of Sorya with the novelist Suong Mak, both of us horribly bored and looking for distraction. Arriving at a new level, we were confronted by the sight of two young Buddhist monks at the food court carrying orange plastic plates of chicken rice. Mak's eyes flashed with outrage. 'It is not polite for them to be here!' he said to me, sotto voce. Going out of his way to walk right past them, he took the time and effort to glare at them pointedly. But the two giggling young monks were completely unaware of the social censure they had brought upon themselves, and they sat down, beaming, to enjoy their store-bought meal. I thought that, as infractions go, this would seem to be a pretty minor one. They were wiry, dark-skinned country boys, perhaps on their first visit to the big city. An illicit chicken lunch, still in the designated hours of monastic eating, seemed a small and not very wicked indulgence.

But not to Mak or some of the other people buzzing around them whispering, laughing and taking photos with their camera phones. So outrageous was this act in Cambodian eyes that Mak took the ultimate refuge. 'They must not be from Cambodia,' he said.

We made our way back down to the Lucky 7 Burger, a singularly unsatisfying fast food joint that emulated all the very worst aspects of McDonald's but added a peculiar extra layer of incredible inefficiency. Never once was I given what I actually ordered at Lucky 7, and I learned to hold on to my receipt in case the meal never actually manifested, which was always a distinct possibility. The reason I loved going, though, was that the dining section was situated right next to a stall that sold the most amazing range of Chinese junk. But this was not the usual assortment of cheap plastics and kitchenware that you might be familiar with. This was an esoteric and ever-changing collection of moderately expensive and ingenious items that I had never before imagined existed.

There were placenta creams, of course, skin-lightening lotions and huge tubs of powdered collagen, along with weight-loss hula hoops and vibrating calf-massagers, but these were all items I'd seen on the streets of Sydney. I was much more fascinated by the non-stop video reel playing on a big-screen TV elevated above the stall that set out in vaguely pornographic detail some of the more intriguing items for sale. Flesh-coloured trunks that came complete with a built-in plump and pert bottom, magnetised reflexology inner soles that seemed to drag dirt and filth from the bottoms of your feet, a heated electronic pad you wear on your face that makes you appear younger, and a breast enlargement pad made from gel-infused silicone complete with a disturbingly realistic nipple.

The screen acted as a hypnotic device, perhaps employing the legendary brain-washing techniques of the Red Chinese to lure in unsuspecting consumers. On the weekends small crowds would gather, and country teenagers would hoot and slap each other whenever the plump-bottomed underwear or pert plastic nipple segments came on. After several burgers I became obsessed with the possibilities of the electrified face-pad, which delivered a series of small electric shocks to the ageing faces of its wearers, thereby rendering them decades younger. I even went along to an in-store demonstration and was wondering if the thirty dollar asking price wasn't, in fact, quite reasonable given the miraculous results.

But the ever-practical Mak quickly hosed some cooling waters on my enthusiasm. 'None of this stuff works,' he growled. 'It is all just junk. They think Cambodian people are stupid, that they will believe whatever they see on TV. And it is not appropriate to show videos of nipples to old ladies.'

We left the air-conditioned confines of Sorya Mall and faced the marauding gangs of tuk tuk drivers and *motoduhps*, all of them calling out and offering monstrously inflated prices. This was part of the theatre of visiting Sorya. If you have the cash to spend a few hours in that place, their thinking goes, then you can afford to pay double for your transport. There was not, however, a single sane paying customer leaving the mall willing to pay the demanded prices, and so elaborate arguments constantly ensued until the most desperate or accommodating driver was found, or until a shopper reached the corner of the street and could wave down someone less rapacious. Fortunately mine is a memorable figure, and so I had established regular drivers who would gladly take me home for something more closely resembling the actual price. And so we hopped into a familiar tuk tuk and went to Wat Botum, Phnom Penh's largest Buddhist temple and the spiritual home to the city's writers. The yard around the Young Writers of Cambodia's office on the grounds of the monastery was always another great standby when you were looking for company or distraction.

And there, sitting on one of the cement benches that were always haunted by tortured poets or earnest young students distributing photocopies of their latest stories, sat the most delightful old woman, talking to one of the small, camp monks that served as the writers' spiritual retinue. 'It's the royal singer!' squealed Mak, clapping his hands in delight. 'You are going to love her!'

HONEYSUCKLE GARLAND

The royal singer was tiny but possessed of enormous presence. She sat upright and wore her silver hair in a bun, which is unusual in Cambodia, where older women normally crop their hair close to their skulls. She had on a fine white lace blouse and a shiny silk sarong. This was obviously a woman who took pride in her appearance. Mak told me all about her: 'She was a singer at the royal palace, before Pol Pot times . . . Now she is back, but as the teacher. So many old songs that only she knows . . . She is the one that the *Apsara* dancers work with.'

Mak and I joined her at the table, and she stood and offered me the most graceful *sampeah* greeting I had ever seen. As we talked, the singer alternately nodded demurely and fixed me with saucy glances. At one stage she stood and, for thirty seconds or so, she sang and made a few spare movements of traditional dance, and she was utterly stunning. With three lines and the elegant swing of an arm she had captured us completely and everyone walking past stopped in silence to see her. At the end of it the monk shrieked and applauded in a display of distinctly un-monk-like behaviour, and the singer smiled and nodded once at us, her eyes disappearing behind soft, plump cheeks. The diva had shown us exactly what she was made of.

Soon more people began to join us. I suspect SMS messages had been sent, and a small party was gathering. I sat with the diva and the monk kept going back and forth to his room to offer us special little gifts and treats. First honeysuckle garlands were offered to us, then a tray of tea and, eventually, a great big basket of fruit, biscuits and chocolates, the kind of elaborate and expensive gift you can buy ready-made at supermarkets especially for offering to monks on special occasions—it was even still wrapped in saffron-coloured cellophane. The sharp-eyed diva swooped in on this, plucking out longans and Czech chocolates and sweet wafer biscuits as she spun story after story to her rapt audience.

The monk decided that photographs were in order, and so we had to pose for a dozen or so taken on his iPhone. After he had examined these he judged that they were not of sufficient quality and so he rushed back to his room to fetch his digital camera. We posed outrageously, the elderly diva, the plump foreigner and the party-animal monk, all of us camping it up, forming different tableaux at the suggestion of bystanders. The temple orphans hung about us, refilling our tea and rushing into the monastery to get cold water for new arrivals. They were very sweet and obviously doted on the monk, who spoke to them with great kindness.

At one stage two of the orphans squatted by him, holding on to his outer robe and laughing sweetly at the stories being told. 'Poor children,' said the monk. 'Both of them know nothing but this monastery. They have lived here since they were babies, no-one at all who knows them or cares for them.'

'Why aren't they monks?' I asked, used to seeing baby monastics at rural temples all over Asia.

'Oh, it is not suitable for them. We don't do that here. Maybe when they are fifteen or sixteen they might choose to be, but for now they are children. We let them be children, go to a normal school. But they know the prayers, of course they do. They have heard them, morning and evening, every day of their lives. I myself have trained them in Pali since the moment they could speak. Show him,' he said, gesturing to the squatting boys. And so they began to pray, in the awkward voices of boys trying to sound deeper, stronger and more serious than is possible. And once again the night grew still around them as everyone stopped to hear their reed-like chants. It was a moment of the most exquisite holiness, and I felt blessed by what I had heard. Afterwards the boys giggled and stole candy from the basket on the table, returning once more to their natural functions. But none of us forgot, after that, their special qualities, born of the saddest of circumstances.

Night began to fall, and the royal singer announced it was time for her to return home. Of course, all of the men in attendance offered to drive her home. I stood to say goodbye and she hugged me, a gesture not common in Cambodia, causing everyone to hoot. Then she turned and made a great routine of going to hug the monk, something absolutely forbidden in Cambodia. Of course she didn't, but this theatrical piece of business caused another great wave of laughter in her audience. I threw my arm over her shoulder and we had a second hug, after which she devised a little dance showing what it was like to hug such a big and fat man. She was thriving on the attention of her spontaneous audience, and I recognised the almost automatic desire to please a crowd felt by all thespians and show-offs. I include myself among their number, and feel the same desperate urge for positive attention.

When I said I had to leave, a softly spoken and muscular young man offered to drive me home. He had been planning to jog around the Independence Monument, but was willing to delay that to offer me a kindness. 'Thank you,' I said, 'that is very kind. I am Walter.'

'Oh yes, I know you,' he responded. 'We became friends on Facebook recently.' This was not an unusual occurrence. Facebook has enormous currency in Phnom Penh, and in many instances it is the principle form of communication between friends. Almost everyone I knew had two or three thousand friends on Facebook. Many had reached their limit of five thousand. But numbers were fluid, because everyone was constantly blocking people who had annoyed them or who had been in some way disloyal. One friend had blocked over a thousand people in a fit of extreme pique, but most had been re-added as they were forgiven.

My new friend was a sports enthusiast with a respect-able and well-paying job in the finance sector. He was one of a new breed of Phnom Penh yuppies who travel abroad (albeit only as far as Vietnam and Thailand), go to the gym and cultivate hobbies in their spare time. His name in Khmer was beautiful, poetic and lyrical, causing me to murmur it to myself over and over again. When I got home I called my friend Panit and asked him what the name meant. 'It means "Fate",' he said. This made it all the more perfect—surely Fate is one of the most beautiful names in the world? 'Too beautiful,' said Panit. 'In fact it is a girl's name. Very strange that his parents called him this. I think it's why he spends so much time building his muscles, to compensate for his name. You sound like you're in love.'

Laughing, I assured Panit that it took more than a lift home to win my heart, and that muscle-bound men were never really my thing anyway. 'Good,' he said, 'because though he has a woman's name, he is a real man.'

EARLY MORNING IN PHNOM PENH

Sina was a monk at one of the biggest monasteries in Phnom Penh, and his vibrant personality, cheeky humour and excellent English saw us become fast friends very quickly. For weeks he had been planning and working on his grandmother's long-life ceremony in Kampong Speu and he had set his heart on my attending. I was to be one of the features of this event, which, he said, would be the grandest ever held at his small village. He left Phnom Penh several days before it began to get things rolling, but he still controlled matters in the city with a military precision via the judicious use of his mobile phone, maintaining constant contact with all of the key players, of whom I had unwittingly become one. Sina's calls could come at any time, but could most be relied on an hour before I woke or forty-five minutes after I had fallen asleep, surely two of the most maddening times to be disturbed.

When the day came for me to travel to the village with a carload of monks I was pretty much up and ready to go shortly after midnight. Like all monkish outings, this one entailed a very early start. I had been instructed to be at Wat Botum, the big royal temple down by the riverside, home of the patriarch of Cambodian Buddhism, at 5 a.m. Thinking I'd get an early start, I was up and strolling towards Wat Botum at four. The streets of Phnom Penh were eerie at this hour.

There was not a single other person up, and as I strolled down the road the occasional tuk tuk driver, asleep in his vehicle at the side of road, would be startled awake and offer up a weary 'Tuk tuk, sir?' before collapsing again into sleep. It was hot already, though still pitch black. How easy it would be, I thought, to be murdered right now, or at least accosted. No-one would ever catch the assailant. Four in the morning might just be the perfect time to commit a crime, I decided. Even the latest night reveler was in bed, and the early birds were yet to venture out. No-one at all sees anything at 4 a.m.

Paul Theroux, in *Ghost Train to the Eastern Star*, describes wonderfully the eeriness of driving through Mandalay in a rickshaw, the ultimate example of vulnerability, an old man in the hands of a stranger in a dark and foreign place. It's exactly how I felt, abandoning myself totally to the potential dangers of this city. There is something about being alone early in the morning in a strange city that heightens one's sensibilities. I can remember other occasions when I have been up early like this, once in Saigon, when I was nearly knocked over by a lonely jogger in the morning gloom, his approach silent, my presence unexpected. We looked at each other with immense surprise mixed with fear, and then we both giggled.

But on this morning I was strolling along singing 'Wouldn't It Be Loverly?' and imagining what it might be like to be a Broadway star. It was hot as hell, the dark and still morning air serving only to underline the fact.

I was too early and the temple gates were closed, and so I went to sit in the park across the road. Fortunately my phone was filled with books and emails and access to Facebook, Twitter and Tumblr, and so I managed to amuse myself in its soft, involving glow. There was not another soul to be seen until finally I heard the low grumble of an approaching motorcycle, a big and expensive one. I glanced up and the driver slowed and glided towards me. I could see it was a fit, older man in sports clothes. His tight, sleeveless T-shirt revealed big, brown biceps. Just a harmless sports-loving pensioner coming out for his morning exercise.

He pulled to a stop right in front of me, turned off the bike and called out: '*Sua s'day*! Hello!'

'*Sua s'day*,' I responded, and at this encouragement he got off his bike and came and sat next to me. Rather too closely next to me, as it happened, but I was used to the friendly proximity between men in Indochina, and so I wasn't bothered. He began to chat away to me in Khmer, and though I kept telling him I couldn't understand he was not bothered at all and kept up his jolly-sounding questions and comments. He was a handsome old fellow, square jawed and solid looking, his expensive sports clothes revealing a heavily muscled body that was unlikely on a man of his age, unless cultivated with care and effort.

His chat became more constantly accompanied with pats and strokes of my person. He ran his hands across my belly repeatedly and laughed. Catching the gist of what he must be saying, I responded in good humour, smiling and nodding and agreeing that yes, I was a fat bastard. The hands then went down to my thighs and set about a peculiar, massaging motion. He was murmuring now, and looked up at me with a smile. Again I responded politely, and at this he reached up, loosened the top few buttons of my shirt and slid his rough hand inside, stroking the hair of my chest, tweaking my nipples and grabbing at my man boobs.

At this I realised we had crossed the boundaries of friendly curiosity and were engaged in something approaching public indecency. I was being fondled at four in the morning by a worryingly muscled sexage-narian in an open, public park. It was with relief that I saw another motorcycle approaching, and my elderly seducer quickly pulled away while I buttoned up. This motorcycle, too, pulled up directly in front of us, and the driver greeted my fit friend. They began to chat in Khmer and there was much laughter and gesturing towards me. This new fellow was younger, more slender and noticeably camp. He got off his bike as well and sat on the bench on the other side of me.

The muscled old fellow smiled at me encouragingly, and no sooner had I smiled in return than the assault began once more, this time from both sides. Buttons were popped and hands were everywhere. The two chatted as they explored and groped various parts of me. After a minute or two my phone rang, and they both sprang back, terrified. I answered the unknown number gratefully, and the young male voice at the other side began to talk to me in a barrage of Khmer. I knew it must be the monk inside the locked monastery, the one

I was meant to meet. I was thoroughly bewildered by now; for the first time since I'd arrived in Cambodia I felt truly lost in a world that couldn't communicate with me. Not knowing what else to do I passed the phone to the sportsman, hoping that he at least could communicate with me in some kind of sign language. He was good with his hands, after all.

Hearing the way he spoke to the person at the other end I knew that it was a monk, and after a little while he hung up and handed the phone back to me. Standing up, he gestured for me to come with him, and then patted the motorcycle seat behind him as he revved up. I don't know what I was thinking as I slid onto the seat behind my amorous friend, especially as he began to drive me down a totally black alleyway running alongside the enormous temple complex. Leaning back into me, one arm resting on my leg, he chatted to me in his gruff, manly purr—was he taking me to some den of iniquity, I wondered? How many dens of iniquity were up and running at 4.30 a.m.? But soon enough we were stopped outside one of the side gates of the temple. It popped open and leaning from the door was a beautiful, monkish head smiling at us.

I rushed inside with enormous relief. Turning back, I thought it would be good manners to say goodbye to my seducer/saviour, and my smile of thanks was rewarded with a movie star wink and flirtatious leer. 'Your friend?' asked the young monk as he locked the gate.

'No,' I said, checking to see my shirt was properly buttoned. 'Just someone I met in the park.'

Once inside the monastery I was led along in the dark shadows with only the cats to scoot across my path and spook me. Cats are ever-present in Cambodian monasteries, living in the nooks and crannies, in tombs and *stupas*, living off the leftovers of the monks' lunches. People here think that cats represent a higher form of rebirth, and that to be cruel to them is wicked. So they live, unloved but unmolested, in a semi-feral state in the temple cemeteries, lurking behind statues of angels and *devadattas*, slender, watchful and yellow-eyed, all belonging to the same, nameless, brown-striped breed. Occasionally one finds its way inside a monk's quarters and is made a pet, but it always remains skinny and suspicious. I never saw a fat cat in Cambodia.

The young monk who was to be my chaperone for the day unlocked one of the dormitories and gestured for me to sit on the plump leather lounge placed somewhat incongruously in the guest area. Leather lounges are not very much in evidence in Cambodia, least of all in the living quarters of religious renunciates. Monks were stumbling about in various states of dishabille, wiping sleepy eyes while they attended to their morning chores, which seemed to consist principally of sweeping. The whole place was coming alive with the sound of coarse brooms sweeping along concrete. I have noticed that people in South-East Asia have a mania for sweeping. My own Vietnamese partner will often sweep the house at strange hours—just before dinner, say, or at midnight when we've arrived back home from a function. But no single community enjoys sweeping as much as the monastic one.

One of the monks set up a little wooden stool and on it he balanced a 1980s-era radio cassette player tuned in to his favourite radio station, which played Khmer classics. There were various shouts of horror and surprise as monks would wander by and, glancing in, see me sitting there unexpectedly. Eventually my young chaperone came back to me, clutching a kitten in one hand and two mobile phones in the other. I didn't know what the plan was, but it looked complicated. The kitten he placed in my lap, beaming at me. That was me taken care of. And since I was now adequately occupied, he began a complicated series of phone calls and text messages, switching between phones. At one stage he even borrowed a phone from one of the other monks.

Then, another phone I hadn't noticed, plugged into the wall behind me to charge, rang and, answering it, the young monk handed it to me. It was Sina, frantic at his distant village in Kampong Speu. 'Oh my God!' he shrieked. 'You are all going to be so late. But I cannot help—a very important monk is coming to collect you.

Just wait until he comes.' And that's what we did, me and the young monk who had no English at all. We just sat across from one another, smiling.

Then, hearing it before I saw it, came the approach of the Very Important Monk. People were screaming outside, monks running up and down the narrow alleyway clutching furniture, pot plants, errant pieces of cement. The Important Monk was coming to the front door, being driven in his ancient Mercedes Benz, leaving about half a centimetre on each side between the car and the buildings. Arriving right outside, he wound down his window in the back seat and leaned right into the room. 'Hello, sir, it's you! I saw you before—you gave that excellent speech about Buddhism on Human Rights day.' I was gratified that my new protector was a fan, though I didn't recognise him. He was very plump and very friendly. In the front seat sat a pretty young man dressed in white robes like a nun, his head shaved. 'Very famous singer,' said the Important Monk, poking the young man in the shoulder. The singer responded with an elegant and wordless *sampeah*.

It was discovered that no-one could enter or leave the car while it was in the alley, unless it was through the windows. So another twenty minutes were taken while the car found a spot with sufficient space to open the doors and let the young monk and I get into the cramped back seat. Just getting out of the monastery took another full twenty minutes, the Mercedes inching its way through the maze of dormitories, shacks and religious buildings, stopping to allow the progress of livestock and people pushing coffee and noodle carts.

No sooner had we turned out of the monastery gates onto a public road than the Important Monk told his driver to stop. 'I'm so hungry, aren't you?' he said, turning to me. Judging by figure alone, if there were any two people likely to be hungry at any given moment it would be the Very Important Monk and myself. I agreed that I hadn't had breakfast either, and so we all climbed out of the car and went into a nearby noodle restaurant. As we ate, one of the young monk's phones buzzed and naturally he took the call. I could hear wild squawking on the other end, and the phone was handed to me.

'Make them leave now! You have no time for breakfast! Oh my God—the day is ruined. You will never be here in time.' It was Sina, of course, now thoroughly distraught. Celebrations were obviously well under way at Kampong Speu, and I could hear a traditional band playing in the background. I promised him that we would leave instantly, and when I hung up the Important Monk ordered a round of iced coffees as he sat back in his chair, picking at his teeth.

But of course we arrived in plenty of time, indeed, before 7 a.m. People always seemed to arrive at the right time in Cambodia, no matter how late they were. When the car pulled up outside the traditional wooden house on stilts, the crowd was thick. As we opened the car doors we had a whole host of video cameras and SLRs thrust in our faces, making it seem as though Lady Gaga had arrived. Sina had hired an entire team of photographers to document the day.

Sina himself pushed his way through the crowd and greeted the visiting monks lavishly with deep bows. Grabbing me and the singer by hand, he thrust us aside into the care of a lean, tattooed man dressed in preposterously fashionable clothes. 'My nephew will take care of you,' said Sina. 'He has just come back from working in Thailand.' I always met such men in country towns across Cambodia, village boys who had been smuggled into Thailand as illegal labourers, spending their youths as abattoir workers or on construction gangs. They could earn double or triple what they would doing the same thing in Cambodia, and the money they sent back kept whole villages functioning. Eventually, though, these young men were caught in periodical swoops on illegal workers, and deported back to Cambodia, where they returned to their villages looking like this man, cocky and well coiffed, possessed of whole new attitudes. They were always plotting how they could get back into Thailand, and many of them managed it, going back two or three times, addicted to the money and the freedom from village life.

The snake-hipped, tattooed one in skinny jeans ferried us in to the transformed space beneath the house. Usually a muddy all-purpose living area, it had been redecorated by Sina into an Oriental paradise, rich with saffron, pink and white polyester drapes, an elaborately painted Buddhist shrine and a richly festooned platform for the monks to sit on. The village elders were all situated closest to this platform and—in the very hottest spot but what was clearly a position of importance—sat the singer and I.

I found it hard to believe that so many elderly people could fit into so small a space, and it was even more miraculous to see Sina weave his way through them, his bright orange robes wrapped tight around him. 'Oh my God!' he called in his characteristic manner. 'Sir, you are sweating like a beast. Poor thing. And it's only going to get hotter.' There was a row of fans trained on the monks' platform, all of them hooked up to a rented generator, for this was a village with no electricity. It was obvious that no expense had been spared for Sina's grandmother's long-life ceremony.

Noticing our discomfort, the Important Monk, who was to deliver the day's religious instruction, ordered one of the fans to be delivered to us, over the heads of the elderly. A pedestal fan, still plugged in and blowing, crowd surfed its way across to us, where it was deposited directly in front of our faces, causing both of us to start weeping from the hot air and incense blown directly into our eyes.

RICE TO SPARE

The ceremony was lengthy and the day was desperately hot. The village women had come wearing their best—white lacy blouses and fine sarongs, a plain costume that had something of an equalising effect. Dressed so alike, most of them with their grey heads cropped, it was impossible for me to tell who was rich and who poor, though later Sina would fill me in on the varying social ranks. The ceremony was a feast for the invited monks, and later for the whole village.

Sina's eye for decorating was roundly being praised, and the religious singer had begun his set, a very specific style of Khmer Buddhist music, to the rapt attention of the village VIPs sitting straight-backed in front of him, their hands clasped in a prayer position. Away from the hot-pink polyester, on a large bamboo platform outside, a troupe of the younger women was busy preparing the lunch.

Each of the guests was given a plate of steamed rice and we lined up at a table that held the monks' bowls. Places in the line were in order of seniority, but because of my peculiarity I was given a spot just below the elder women of the village, a quite elevated position. The women pinched me and giggled as they showed me what to do, taking a handful of rice and throwing it into each monk's begging bowl. At the end of this was another, smaller, table on which were a half-dozen bowls made of woven banana leaves. These were to be offered to the hungry ghosts and village spirits, and had to be filled as well. Indeed, much of the celebration, including the music supplied by a small travelling orchestra, was intended as a special offering to the village spirits, who are always present in the thoughts of rural Cambodians. Soon, each and every container was piled high with rice, and the line had some way to go yet: there were still the middle-aged to come, then the young parents and finally the young adults, who could only pitch a few grains of rice onto each collapsing tower. Of course, the opulence and waste was all part of the ceremony, to prove that the host had rice to spare.

While I wandered around the outside in relative comfort as the ceremonies went on and on, Sina would occasionally send for me, and I would be dragged unwillingly into the tremendous heat of the main celebration area. The monks sat on their platform for hour after hour, stoically performing their duties and being rewarded at the end with enormous gift baskets wrapped in cellophane, containing all of the items it was thought monks would need. I was always interested to see what these were, and I noticed these had religious robes, a small packet of Omo, a jar of Ovaltine, Choco

Pie biscuits from Korea, a tube of Deep Heat, instant noodles and other consumables. There was, as well, a generous cash donation in a discreet envelope.

The time came for the VIP monk to leave, and he called me to join him in the car. Sina, however, told him that this wasn't the plan—I was in, apparently, for the long haul. So I regretfully waved at the Very Important Monk and the doleful ceremonial singer as they made their way back to Phnom Penh in the air-conditioned comfort of a Mercedes Benz. Never had someone else's departure been so keenly felt. Sina had a full afternoon planned for me, and soon we were on our way, part of a full Cambodian village immersion experience that I hadn't planned on.

Back at the ceremony the village poor and elderly were leaving, and each was given a party favour as they left. This was a small sack of rice wrapped in a new cotton *krama*. On top was a flower, some incense and an envelope filled with riel, the Cambodian currency that I almost never encountered in Phnom Penh, US dollars being much preferred. The widows of the village were numerous, and many of them relied on parties and ceremonies such as this to survive, as it was customary to make an offering to the poor. Blind women, ancient women, the disabled and the mentally ill, all were brought to Sina and then me to receive a special blessing.

As a crowd thronged around me I began to feel like a fraudulent faith healer. Old women touched my arms, pinched my cheeks and held my soft hands up against their rough, wrinkled faces. 'They love you and want to talk to you,' cried Sina, above the heads of the crowd. 'They say you are fat and beautiful.' And so I gave in to my rock star moment, in the name of international friendship.

But my official duties were only just beginning. For the rest of the afternoon Sina took me on a complete tour of the village, visiting everyone. Palm sugar farmers, shamans and landlords all supplied us with sticky cakes and hot glasses of soft drink as a horrendous headache made its way further and deeper into my consciousness. We toured farms, and at one stage I was made to strip and bathe in the river with the cowherds. We visited thatched shacks and beautiful wooden houses on stilts. Sometimes, coming into a new house, I would discover the exact same group of people I thought I'd been talking to several houses ago. 'Oh yes, that's them,' said Sina. 'But they were just visiting there. This is their house.'

At one place a cheery old lady was produced as an item of curiosity. 'Never married!' cried Sina, waiting for my shocked expression. When I simply smiled in an embarrassed way, Sina pressed the meaning of her uniqueness. 'You understand, she is not crazy, not sick, not a nun. She just never married. The only woman in the village ever to live like that.' While the people around us murmured and chatted about this incredible phenomenon, the woman sat and smiled, content in her local celebrity. Sina said something that made everyone shriek with laughter. 'I said that maybe she should marry you, because you are a bachelor.' The beloved spinster smiled indulgently at all of us, and shot me a conspiratorial wink.

When the time came for us to leave the village, the booked car never arrived. Sina made a dozen animated and loud calls, but to no avail. 'No-one is coming,' he said, his face creased in shame and fury. 'People in Cambodia are not reliable! The driver found another customer and went to Phnom Penh without us.' This caused something of a panic. It was dark now, and the villagers were stuck with an important and difficult guest. Sina's religious vows meant that he could not eat after noon, but for me a suitably grand dinner had to be arranged.

I heard a strangled squawk and knew that chicken would be served. And so it was, along with tiny fried canned sausages, a mountain of rice, slices of watermelon and green mango, and the inevitable plastic cup of hot 7Up. By now I was installed on a large wooden platform bed set up under a *beng* tree outside the village shop. I had the distinct feeling I was outstaying my welcome, my presence now a source of stress more than excitement. Only the cousin who had visited Thailand remained constant, though he, too, had lost some interest. By now he was hungover, having gotten himself so completely drunk in the morning. After dinner he pulled off his shirt and fell asleep on the platform next to me, offering me the solace, at least, of knowing he was nearby, and still probably fulfilling his duty.

Sina ran from house to house borrowing mobile phones and seeking out new sources of transport. His own phone had gone flat after the excesses of the day. Occasionally he would loom up out of the impossibly dark night and cry, 'Oh, sir! How bad I feel! We must get you out of here.' Finally, at around 10 p.m., we heard the rattle of a car approaching on the rutted village road. 'Our car is here,' called Sina from somewhere in the night. By this stage I had rolled over next to my Thai protector and was snoring contentedly. The village men assembled by torchlight and the minivan was slowly loaded with the most incredible assortment of goods. Carpets, chairs, statues, vast cooking pots. Everything used in the ceremony had been borrowed from someone else, and the time had come to return it.

A place was found among the detritus of the day for Sina to sit, and then for me. Once we had been given our cramped spaces, the van was then opened up for passengers. It seems that quite a few people had somewhere to go that was on our way, and some of them had serious stuff to carry. Once the van had acquired a thoroughly dangerous load, we set off into the night, our bodies heaving up off the seats at each bump on the dreadful dirt roads.

The drive took hours, stopping constantly to let off passengers or return property. By the time we were entering Phnom Penh, Sina was sound asleep, his head resting on one of the triangular ceremonial pillows intended for monks to lean on. I begged for them to leave me outside my hotel, though this meant Sina couldn't get out to say his usual elaborate goodbyes. It was improper for monks to be seen hanging about hotels, particularly ones like mine.

The night security guards were all asleep in front of the cars and motorbikes they were guarding, having discreetly draped them with covering cloths so no-one could identify their owners and question their various assignations inside my hotel. I pulled my phone from my pocket and glanced at the time. It was just after midnight.

MY HEART BELONGS TO DADDY

No-one I knew seemed to have a father. Indeed, a good number of my friends had no parents at all, or had absentee parents who had, at some point in their childhood, left them at an institution and only turned up intermittently to ask for money. In a society as damaged as Cambodia, deadbeat parenting was the norm, and thousands, maybe millions, of people have grown up institutionalised and more or less angry at their blood relatives.

My friend Chanphal, for instance, had been brought up by his mother and her sisters. Exquisitely sensitive, literary and dreamily romantic, at some stage in his childhood, Chanphal heard that his father had once sold ice cream, and he cherished this wonderful detail. 'I used to think, if only he was around, I could eat all the ice cream I wanted,' he told me. 'Then, one day when I was eight or nine, this strange man turned up at my school, claiming to be my father. I took one look at him and ran away—he was nothing like what I had dreamed about.' Much later, when Chanphal was twenty-two, his father hunted him down again, and this time the two met for a meal. This man was sad: old and haggard, he had become a decrepit alcoholic, making his living as a *motoduhp* driver in a small regional city.

'We had nothing to say to one another,' said Chanphal. 'So we ate in silence. At the end I slipped him some money and he drove away on his terrible old bike. That night I cried myself to sleep. Was this what I would become? But now, strangely, I feel like I miss him. I feel like I want to help him, but whenever I ask around, no-one knows where he is. He hasn't been seen for years. Everyone says he is a *motoduhp* driver somewhere in Kompong Cham, that he's a drunk.' His eyes became teary at the thought, and at the memory of this sad man he only remembered seeing twice in his entire life.

My monk friend Sina was forced to enter the monastery at a young age after the death of his father. 'He was not a good man,' said Sina. 'He was the town drunk, a gambler. He had so many children, but he never cared for us, and my mother was disabled and left us to wander the village like chickens.'

'I was the oldest,' explained Sina, 'and as soon as I could work out what was going on I realised that it was my responsibility to care for the other children. We stole, we worked, we went to live at strangers' houses, anything to keep us alive. Finally I saw that by entering the monastery I could keep the younger ones fed with the little bit of food and money I could save there.' And there he was, in his thirties and still clearly a monk-supporter, a not-unusual role in Cambodia. Living in a big monastery in Phnom Penh, he could slowly save up the donations he received from lay people and then re-distribute them among his needy siblings and his poor, mad mother.

I seemed to be in a nation of absent fathers. My friend Kimly had grown up in an orphanage, though his mother was alive. 'She was just never interested,' he told me, a slight edge of bitterness in his voice. Our mutual friend Sambath was another orphanage child. He too had a family that he met occasionally, but they were too poor and had too many children, and so he had been abandoned to the care of an orphanage. Hearing the complex stories of these quasi-orphans helped me realise why international adoption is such a minefield of potential grievance and conflict. Though they might not see him from one year to the next, Sambath's parents still saw him as their property, and once he was an adult and earning a wage, they expected him to contribute to the family finances.

This kind of fundamental absence of the most basic kind of love, experienced by so many, may explain the Khmer passion for romantic stories and ideas of love. Most of my friends were single, but harboured great and unrealistic hopes of finding a perfect, storybook partner. Chanphal, for example, was intent on finding true love, and in its absence he wrote romantic stories, poems and songs that were immensely popular. Though most Cambodians disapproved of homosexuality almost as a reflex, they were fascinated to hear about my own twenty-plus year relationship, urging me to retell all of the most romantic moments and declaring, over and over again, 'You have been a lucky man. You have what we all dream of.'

But perhaps my seeking to site the root of this romantic obsession in the ruins of tragedy and disunity is the result of my own unexamined romanticism. The Cambodians are constantly romantic about most things: history, childhood, religion, nature; all are subjected to overblown allusions at every turn, though these outbursts are so unaffected, so lacking in cynicism, that they can be genuinely moving. Chanphal would often talk to me about the great innocent pleasures of growing up in the provinces and swimming naked in the river—this is such a common motif, and one that I have witnessed. He talked about seeing the moon—'I love to see the moon in the provinces—you cannot see it properly in Phnom Penh.' Chanphal also told me that when he was a boy he had converted briefly to Christianity in order to take advantage of the free English lessons. He loved church, especially the singing, and he still remembers all the songs today. But ultimately the exclusive nature of the theology he was taught made no sense to him, so he dropped it.

While driving through Cambodia's provinces you notice that most schools have shrines to the Buddha in the front yard, a fact that sits uneasily for someone brought up in the secular system. But Cambodia's government makes no claims to be secular. Except for the brief period of the Khmer Rouge, Buddhism has been Cambodia's state religion for the best part of 800 years, and still claims 95 per cent of Cambodia's population as its followers. Each morning school children pledge allegiance to the Buddha, the king and the nation, and it's best not to challenge any of these institutions while you are there.

PHNOM PENH'S
OLDEST HOOKER

Being drunk is dangerous for me. I am a man who is unusually uninhibited, and after a couple of beers those few inhibitions I do possess tend to slip away with remarkable ease. And so I become dangerous. Not in any violent way, mind—far from it. But in the 'wouldn't it be terrific if we all went to my place and continued this party' kind of way, or the 'let's go to a karaoke bar so I can do my famous rendition of Cher's "Believe"' kind of way. I become dangerously jolly.

So it was, late one night, that I met Sam, the man my friends later came to call, rather cruelly, 'Phnom Penh's oldest hooker'. We were all at the infamous Blue Chilli bar, a Phnom Penh institution that is exactly what a gay bar would be like if you established one in the garage of a rented holiday home. I was plastered, and all of my friends almost equally so, and into our group came Sam. I will admit that, with his big, muscular build and gruff masculinity, his dark skin and his rough face, I had assumed that Sam, a man at least in his forties, was a staff member, perhaps even a cleaner. Phnom Penh nightlife favours the young, and anyhow the older generation of gay Cambodians, having grown up in a very different age, were discreet to the point of invisibility, and it was said that most of them were married with children and couldn't stay out late. So places like the Blue Chilli were always filled up with handsome young men on the make and people like my friends, an emerging generation of young gay professionals creating their own kind of middle class, emulating the values, interests and social strata of gay life in the West.

Sam laughed with us, drank our drinks, ate our peanuts and edged ever closer to me, the only non-Cambodian in the group. When he got up to visit the toilet my disapproving friends leaned in and said, 'What does that strange old man want with us? Be careful and don't talk to him. He's probably a gangster. We'll make him go away.' But Sam came back and confidently pushed everyone aside and sat next to me, throwing a comradely arm around my shoulder and picking up the nearest cocktail, which he downed.

'A nice big, fat man like you,' he said warmly. 'We don't get many in here. You're what a man should be. Not like these thin little kids.' At this he gestured at my friends, all of them scrupulously slender. They glared back at him, and began to pepper him with questions in Khmer.

'Tell us, grandpa, are you a *motoduhp*?'

'Are you getting the next round of drinks, uncle?'

'We young ones must certainly listen to a silver-haired fellow like you.'

But Sam ignored them all and fixed me with a disarmingly white and healthy smile. We all kept drinking. There was dancing on the bar (not by me) and, at some late point, a rather unfortunate drag show, but it was all becoming a blur. My friends began to check their watches. For all of their outrageous sophistication, most still lived at the beck and call of clock-watching mothers, aunts and landladies, and none dared stretch their curfews too far. One by one they left, until there was just a few of us at the bar and the staff began wiping down surfaces and looking at the dregs of the evening hopefully. A substantial tip, and possibly even a commercially beneficial assignation, could be charmed out of any drunk customer this late in the night.

'You're coming with me,' said the uncouth Sam, pulling me out into the humid night. At this point I really began to believe that he was in fact a tuk tuk driver: he certainly looked like one. But, handing a ticket to the attendant, he was delivered with an expensive-looking new motorcycle, and we drove off into late-night Phnom Penh, looking for noodles. As Sam saw it, this was far from the end of the evening. His appetite for alcohol was prodigious, and he downed two beers while he ate an enormous plate of fried noodles, and I sat there queasily in the ghastly fluorescent light shining from the mobile stall, breathing in the grease. 'I know some other places we could go to drink,' he growled in his friendly manner, 'or we could go to my cousin's house and play cards.'

I did not want to go and play cards. Amateur gambling is a very dangerous activity for any tourist in Cambodia, and, as a young man, I had lost some dollars going banker for a friend at a spontaneous gambling session in rural Thailand. I knew things could get ugly fast, if they hadn't already been specifically designed to fleece the unsuspecting tourist. Gambling and drinking were the overweening sins of Cambodia, and the papers every morning were filled with the results of each. People with nothing regularly gambled away all they had—motorcycles, houses, children, wives. I had just read of a woman who had actually imprisoned and enslaved a group of Vietnamese gamblers who weren't good for their debts. The Cambodians took their gambling seriously.

Sam looked hurt when I so vehemently turned down the cards, and also begged off extra drinks because I was beginning to feel so out of sorts. 'I think I'd like to just go home,' I said, now feeling almost sober in my sickness.

At this, Sam perked up. 'Oh yes, we'll go to your home, a great idea.' He made a great show of paying for the noodles, which came to less than a dollar, and then we climbed back on to his bike and I gave him the directions to my place. Pulling up outside my hotel, I clambered off and thanked him for his company. 'No need to say goodbye here,' said Sam, 'I'll come up to your room.'

I felt nothing but alarm at the thought of this man in my room. He was tall and big-framed and so solidly muscled that his thin cotton shirt stretched at the seams whenever he turned his torso or lifted his arms. Even if he had nothing but a nightcap in mind—a fact I seriously doubted—there was no way I could handle anything that Sam decided to do. 'No, really,' I begged. 'I don't feel well at all. I want to be sick. We'll meet up another time—I really have to go to bed now.' Sam looked confused and slightly panicked at this, his helmet off but his thick legs still straddling his bike.

'But I won't charge you much,' he said, 'seventy dollars only, because I like you.'

I became panicked at this. My friends had been right. Sam had had nothing but profit in mind and was, indeed, the world's most unlikely male prostitute. Fortunately the security guards at my hotel were great pals who I tipped lavishly, and sensing some conflict they gathered around us. Confident that none of them could speak English, Sam dismounted from his bike and walked me into the hotel lobby.

'I tell you what,' he said, 'for you only fifty, because we've had such a good time tonight and you are my style of man.' The camp young night attendants at the hotel desk stared at us in disbelief. Their English was perfectly good, and it was absolutely clear to them what was going on. My previously spotless reputation was being tarnished right before their eyes.

'No,' I said, my mouth dry with panic at the potential for this situation to go horribly wrong. Why had I been so stupid in allowing this stranger to go as far as he had?

'Please,' he said, grabbing me hard by the arm to prevent my walking away. 'Thirty dollars, you won't regret it. There are parts of me you don't know about that you will love. Please. I have nowhere else to go tonight.' But the desk attendants had called out to the security guards, and they ambled in, shooting amused glances to each other.

'No!' I said, pulling myself away from him and heading to the stairwell. 'I feel sick and I need to sleep.' Two of the security guards slid in behind me and stopped the desperate Sam from following me. Pausing, I turned around and, fishing in my wallet, I pulled out a twenty and handed it to him. He snatched at it angrily.

'Don't give him money, sir!' called the queeny night porter. 'He is a bad man.'

As I rushed up the stairwell I heard Sam's deep, rough voice echoing behind me. 'Please, brother,' he called, 'let me stay. For you I will give it free, you are so cute and sweet.' Reaching my room, I fumbled with the key at the door, half expecting a drunken and crazed Sam to come barrelling up behind me. But finally, my heart pounding, I had the door open, and, just before I slammed it shut I heard Sam's impossibly manly voice rumbling up the stairwell.

'So fat, so lovely,' he called.

TALK OF THE TOWN

The weather had taken a much hotter turn than I could ever have expected. Cambodia's legendary heat is really not to be underestimated, and that is precisely what I had done. Though I retained my sense of propriety by wearing jeans at formal events and when I went out with friends, I was sneaking around town in the afternoons and early evenings in shorts, feeling terribly risqué. I must stress that my shorts finished somewhere below my knee, but there is no underestimating the level of disapproval most people in Cambodia heap upon shorts. One of my friends even wore trousers to bed, so thoroughly did he scorn the idea of exposing one's legs.

Being in a prim state of mind, I had not packed many pairs of shorts when I came away, and I found myself in need of more. There was a seamstress just downstairs, but my encounter with her proved hugely frustrating. She overcharged me monstrously, took three days longer than promised, and then sent up several pairs that were woefully below par: some had not been stitched properly, others were unhemmed, in one she'd left out the elastic. It was such a bad and botched job that I couldn't imagine it was anything other than a deliberate slight. This plunged me into a depression which almost had me booking an early ticket home. It seemed so representative of my life in Cambodia, where everything was a struggle, everything had to be fought and argued for, and nothing could be guaranteed.

'Does she take no pride in her work?' I roared at poor Mak, who had the misfortune to visit me in the midst of my funk. He attempted no defence of the maligned seamstress, standing there and taking my savage denunciation with a calm impassivity that made me even more frustrated. 'How can the woman live with herself?' I screamed, really wanting to know the answer. Despite my friendliness and quietness, my tendency to overtip and my real willingness to connect with people, I felt snubbed in my neighbourhood, and frequently ill used. At the little shop where I bought my most pressing supplies, I was charged three different sets of prices, according to who was serving me. It didn't seem a way to treat a good customer who returned again and again with the same order.

My hotel was situated in its own small entertainment district in an obscure corner of downtown Phnom Penh. I was surrounded by nightclubs, karaoke bars and restaurants, but they were all frequented almost exclusively by locals, so my presence was cause for comment and speculation. I had to be methodical and judicious in how I frequented the local restaurants.

I needed to establish a pattern of fairness, whereby I was seen to eat at each with the same frequency. My judgement was always being questioned, however. One night, leaving the seafood noodle restaurant with a friend, the proprietress of the fried rice restaurant scooted over and demanded to know why I had eaten noodles twice in a short period, bypassing her own establishment. I begged forgiveness, and the next day I made sure I ate fried rice, though I was treated frostily by staff and owners alike. I decided it might be prudent to keep a spreadsheet showing exactly when I had eaten and where, and I maintained it carefully till the end of my stay. It was obvious that what I did and with who was more or less common knowledge.

There was also the small matter of sex, a subject about which the Khmer are notoriously squeamish. My presence as an unaccompanied white male was always being questioned. Whenever I had female friends come to see me I always made sure we chatted in the guest area on the ground floor of the hotel. This impressed the hotel staff, but all the local shopkeepers saw was a woman leaving and entering and occasionally getting into a tuk tuk with me, and so my reputation as a lothario began to grow. The possibility of my being sexually uninterested in women seemed to occur to no-one, even though I was seen much more often in the company of flamboyant transsexuals than the sombre and plain Buddhist girls who were my friends.

The heat, my lack of language skills, and my friends' conviction that every single thing I wanted to do was either dangerous or impossible, meant that I was becoming isolated. I realised that I needed to be saying yes more often, that I needed to be having adventures, going out more. I needed to consciously remind myself of these things each and every day, or else I could find myself in the middle of Cambodia sitting in my air-conditioned room all day reading books about Cambodia. The curse of the bookish is that we frequently prefer the printed version to the reality.

I spent my hot days all too frequently in a slightly depressive state, bearing an incredible sense of time wasted, of whole days lost. To what? I really needed to try harder, push myself more. My lack of productivity made me feel stupid and the whole journey I was engaged in, pointless. I was beginning to actually hate myself, and the greater my self-loathing grew, the less I could do with my day. The country was making its slow transition into the wet season, and every forty-eight hours or so we would experience a deluge in the late afternoon that stopped the city.

Caught out in the rain one such wet afternoon, I ducked into an alcove in an alleyway in an attempt to stay dry. In doing so, I gashed my arm open on a piece of rusty barbed wire someone had once strung up there like a Christmas garland, a protective device to stop loiterers like me. Standing there bleeding in the hot rain, filthy water splashing back up at me from the flooded drains, all I could think of was tetanus. My last tetanus injection had been when I was eight. Could I expect its protective effects to last thirty-three years?

'Never fear, brother, you are protected,' said Panit, reminding me that one of the specific purposes of the magical painted talisman his mother had given me was protection from cuts. Fortunately the two bottles of cheap cologne I kept in my bag at all times came to good use, and I alternately swilled out the deep cut with Black Knight and then Eternal Love. The sting was violent, but the dominant notes were orange-flower and straw-berry, so the filthy and dangerous little alcove where we were trapped became positively fragrant. Fishing the talisman from my bag, Panit pressed it to my wound and whispered a few lines in Pali, the ancient Buddhist language. 'You are fine now,' he assured me.

I was sceptical. Once the worst of the rain was over we made our way back home, and I walked the four hot floors back up to my room. I swallowed some painkillers and a couple of sleeping pills. If the cold shakes and agonies of tetanus were going to overtake me, I wanted to pre-empt them a little. Naturally enough, I fell into my bed and into a deep sleep. When I woke up late the next morning I checked my arm and the bloody, ragged wound of the previous evening seemed to be the merest scratch. There was no pain, no swelling, just the lingering odour of Black Knight. I called Panit and told him about my miraculous healing.

'No miracle,' he assured me. 'It is the job of the talisman. Easy for the magic to work with you. I know for a fact you've never slept with anyone's wife.'

CHANPHAL

Chanphal is a gentle, quiet and unassuming man who is one of Cambodia's most successful novelists and song-writers. He is, in fact, a celebrity, though in his humility he is never recognised on the streets. The quantity of his Facebook followers could fill a small city, but in real life he maintains a small and close-knit group of friends who are compatible with his shyness. One of his passions is to take cruises along the river, and so I agreed to come along, thinking it would be some kind of floating restaurant that serves the tourist crowd. But Chanphal's affairs were altogether different.

I loved the whole ritual of it, and the haphazard collection of friends, interesting people, artists, musicians and sometimes feuding lovers who would inevitably turn up. We would gather at one corner of the Old Market where a woman had an incredibly popular stall that sold a large variety of Chinese desserts. This was how our meals would always start, on land with a selection of brightly coloured and teeth-jarringly sweet desserts topped with warm coconut milk. Normally at the dessert stall there was not a seat to be had, especially not as our group expanded, and I frequently had to stand up to eat mine. I discovered things I had no idea were delicious: boiled winter melon served with crushed ice and drizzled with condensed milk; sweet sticky rice and black beans; sugary dumplings filled with sesame paste. As the various drifters, bohemians and ne'er-do-wells turned up, the conversation would become increasingly raucous, and any pretence at maintaining English was given up. I cursed myself for not learning to speak Khmer, as I'd promised myself I would. Why hadn't I applied myself over the previous year, when I had known that I would be coming to Cambodia for an extended period?

We purchased our meal from the old market, surprisingly delicious banquets pieced together from whatever street-food sellers were hanging about. Sticky rice, thick chunks of dried fish, grilled chicken and mysterious barbecued meatballs that no-one could vouch for were the staple. The stalls were really outdoor buffets, and everything was served to us in slender plastic bags with bamboo chopsticks wrapped at the top in a dangerously complicated manner. While all my friends could elegantly untwist them and begin eating, I engaged in a dangerous and filthy battle which I always lost, my front splashed with Chinese sausages, little dried and barbecued whitebait and two different types of pickled cucumber.

Then the group that had assembled would head down to the docks and negotiate the hire of a wooden pleasure boat. I was always assured that the boat owners were quite reasonable in their charges, but invariably, upon seeing me, their prices began to shift. I am forever doomed to be an object of interest, a focal point, wherever I travel. I am noticed, and it is impossible for me to slide into anonymity, no matter where I am in the world. I will always be seen, I will always be commented on. I am invariably the biggest, the oddest looking, the baldest, the fattest. This visibility is a function of my existence that I simply must accept and live with. Sometimes it can be exhausting. And at others it is an enormous asset. But sometimes I wish I could just slip quietly by in the crowd.

Unnervingly, my presence at the makeshift wooden docks was frequently noted, not just by the boatmen, but by friends passing by. I would receive messages on my phone: 'I saw you by the river,' or 'So many friends! No wonder you never have time to see me.' It was at these times that I was aware of just how small Phnom Penh was, and how I could never, no matter how long I stayed there, hope to disappear into it as an invisible resident.

The boat would putter up and down the river while we ate on the upper deck and abstemiously sipped at sweating, warm cans of Pepsi, the hot breeze blowing in our faces. Our alfresco meals were exceedingly delicious and everyone ate with relish. Each time, Chanphal would declare: 'You are eating like the poor people tonight!'

The river spoke to Chanphal, a gentle, fatherless boy who wrote bittersweet love songs, though he was terminally single, and was inclined to slip into reveries about the moon and flowers and village life without sounding at all affected. Chanphal was a romantic, and everything he saw was mediated through this romantic vision. But the counterpoint to the romantic worldview must always be the presence of monsters, and Chanphal was a great believer in ghosts, spirits and the magical. We shared this common interest.

Gazing down at the water, both of us hot and sweaty despite the breeze blowing from the river, he asked me suddenly about mermaids. 'What do you think,' he said, smiling, 'of people who say that there are whole worlds underneath the water? My family is part Chinese, and I grew up with stories of fish who turn themselves into women.' This was an uncanny topic of conversation, because all day I had been reading a novel by the Chinese writer Julie O'Yang based on this very myth. 'All of the rivers and lakes in Cambodia are inhabited by fish spirits and dragons,' he explained. 'It is something I have heard ever since I was a boy. When I am on the river I always spend some time like this, looking out at the water and praying for them.'

When we arrived back on land Chanphal offered to drive me home on the back of his motorcycle. 'There is something I want to show you,' he said. Turning a few corners, we stopped outside a large statue of Ganesh erected in recent years in a tiny park at the end of Monivong Boulevard, right near the Central Market where the taxis wait. It was stranded there on a triangular piece of land, the grass growing green and lush around it. Chanphal had been in my room and seen my little shrine on a corner of my desk, a cluster of Ganeshas surrounded by colourful crystals and garlands of honeysuckle and jasmine. Knowing of my interest, this was a place he'd been saving for me.

In the evening no-one at all was at the shrine, and we walked silently across the grass and stood before the tall and leanly modern rendering of the elephant-headed God. Here, right in the middle of Phnom Penh, was a memorial to Cambodia's Hindu past and to its rich and complicated mystical traditions. We knelt at the small platform before the statue with nothing to offer but our hopes and our prayers. And these we sent up into the hot Phnom Penh night.

THE YOUNG WRITER

The whole reason for my new engagement with modern Cambodia was the young novelist Suong Mak. I had read about him in the Western media. He was the author of a scandalous novel that was thought to be the first ever in Khmer to talk about gay male relationships. It didn't take me long to hunt him down. Thanks to the marvel of Facebook, I managed to send him a message, and he responded quickly.

Then, one day when I was lounging about my room hoping for some adventure, I received a text message: 'This is Suong Mak—meet me at Sorya Mall.' This was too exciting to be true, and I leaped into a tuk tuk and headed down there. We hadn't arranged an actual spot to meet in the multilevelled shopping mall, and so I wandered about looking into the face of every moderately poetic young man who came by. None returned any looks of recognition, though some started to follow me around. Then I saw, descending the escalator, an exceedingly slender man who looked more like a boy. He smiled and waved and here, at last, was the scandalous, culture-changing and globally acclaimed writer. I would never have picked him out in a crowd.

We went to have ice cream—always my meeting strategy of choice in Phnom Penh—and I quickly fell under the spell of this enchanting man. He is a strange but quite wonderful person, fragile. In his photographs he was plain, but in real life he is in fact quite beautiful, with huge, expressive eyes and a winningly conspiratorial manner. I flirted with the man who took our order and Mak, watching the interaction, slapped my hand as the waiter walked away and said, 'How bad you are!' I knew then that we would become friends.

Mak is immensely cultured, and almost instantly we began a conversation about the *Ramayana*, of which he knew a great deal. This Indian classic is an important part of the imagery and content of Cambodian theatre, art and dance, and scenes from it can be found etched into the walls of Angkor Wat. Mak knew these murals well, and spoke beautifully and entertainingly of them, all the while maintaining that he knew nothing about religion. I must admit that my first thought, rather shamefully was, 'How useful this person will be—knowledgeable and yet fun.' This is a pre-eminent sin of writers, I think; so often we see people first as providers of content. I was also impressed by his humility, by the lightness with which he dispensed his knowledge.

Mak shuffled through his bag and brought out a nice-looking digital camera. 'We must take a photograph of our first meeting,' he said. When I admired the camera, an item of technology not within the means of most Cambodians, he looked a little guilty and said, 'Yes, it is my one indulgence, and it caused me much heartache.'

'Heartache?' I asked, wondering how a camera could be the source of emotional conflict in anyone's life.

'Yes!' said Mak. 'It almost ruined my life. You see, ever since I was a boy I have dreamed of having a camera. Finally, in 2009 the SEA Games came to Laos, and I found a job there for a week as one of the official greeters. At the end of it I had earned $400—a fortune, the most I had ever had handed to me. I knew instantly what I wanted to do. I spent the entire amount on a Sony digital camera—the thing I had always dreamed of owning. I was so happy to have it—it would help me with my work, to record memories, and to make my blog more exciting and interesting.

'You will laugh. Coming from a rich country, but until then I had doubted I could ever have my own camera. I was twenty-four and this was my first ever. I was so proud and happy that I rushed home and did a blog post about it. My blog is very popular in Cambodia, and so many of my readers sent me congratulations and comments, which made me even happier. But then, that night, I received an email from my little brother. He too had read the post, and he was furious. It was a stinging email, accusing me of greed, materialism, of disloyalty to our mother—how could I spend so much money on a single, frivolous purchase? I knew he was right, of course, and so I was devastated for weeks. I couldn't take the camera out of its box for shame.'

Despite the modern content, there was something mythic and eternal in this tale. Was there any redemption, I asked?

'Oh yes,' said Mak, smiling now. 'All was forgiven. My brother Tola sent me a message the next month begging my forgiveness for speaking to me like that and hoping that the camera was proving useful. He is a sweet and kind boy who could never stay angry at me. And now, when I am back in Cambodia, he uses it more than me.'

I laughed at this, delighted at the good grace and closeness of the two. 'Oh, I hope I can meet your brother,' I said. 'He sounds adorable.'

Mak paused for just a moment and then said, 'You will meet him. I only worry about one thing.'

'What?' I asked.

'That you will fall in love with him. My brother, you see, is impossibly beautiful.'

I laughed at this phrase, but discovered, upon meeting Tola, that it was in fact perfectly true. He was preternaturally handsome, and as solicitous, witty and funny as his brother. Something had blessed the Suong brothers. Two small, fatherless village boys had grown up into extraordinary men, one brilliant, one beautiful and both ridiculously charming.

Suong Mak had conceived of the idea of becoming a writer when he was fifteen. Over a few months he would sit down every evening after his homework was finished and carefully write out a ghost story he'd dreamed up in a special exercise book bought for him by an indulgent mother who could ill afford such luxuries. Cambodians delight in ghost stories, so it seemed a natural genre to begin in. He wrote the story methodically and carefully in pencil, worried about making mistakes and thereby wasting valuable paper. When it was finished he gave it to his mother to read, and she finished it quickly the next day, going back to it in the quiet periods between customers at her noodle stall in Kompong Cham. 'It's very good,' she told her pleased son when she got home that night. 'But what do we do with it now?' Neither of them knew what to do with a manuscript, and so Mak put it in a box by his bed and wondered at his monumental foolishness and waste of time. Skinny schoolboys who lived in thatch-roofed houses in rural Cambodia did not write novels.

Then, some weeks later, the family was listening to a radio program in the evening, and being interviewed was a successful Cambodian novelist and publisher. 'That's the sort of person we need to meet,' said Mak's mother, taking a careful note of his name. The next afternoon she visited the tiny bookstall outside the Kompong Cham high school and purchased two of that man's books, using up almost all of the profits for the day. She read his books carefully, deciding that they were no better than her son's effort. Mak read them too, with some awe. They were the first new books that had ever been in his house, and what's more, he had heard the author speaking on the radio, and so he already revered him. He noticed that on the back cover of the books was printed the address of the publishing house in Phnom Penh. He pointed this out to his mother, and the next morning she woke him at 4 a.m., already dressed in her best sarong. 'Wake up, son, and get that book of yours. We are going to meet the author.'

They stood by the side of their dusty village road, waiting for a truck to pick them up. These trucks filled their back trays with passengers and took them to Phnom Penh in the heat, wind and, all too often, rain, all of them totally exposed to the elements. It was the cheapest form of transport, a fraction of what the derelict buses cost. Fortunately the weather held out for Mak and his mother and, after four or so hours, they were dropped off on the outskirts of the city. His mother had packed two little parcels of sticky rice to keep them going for the day. 'The market people will give us water, if we ask them nicely,' she said with false bravado.

It had been many, many years since his mother had visited Phnom Penh, and she had no idea of the layout of the city, or even of where they'd been dropped off. Mak himself had only been once. As a small boy, in the days before his father had fallen ill, the two of them had caught the bus to visit Wat Phnom, which Mak had been obsessed with after reading about it in a children's comic book. This comic book was an antique, a survivor of the pre-Pol Pot days, and it described Wat Phnom as something of a paradise on earth, the surrounding park containing a fun fair and a zoo and people selling spun sugar and barbecue. Mak was desperate to see the zoo, and he regularly begged his father to take him to it.

When they finally got to Wat Phnom, they discovered that the fun fair and the zoo were long gone, all of them destroyed by the Khmer Rouge, who had eaten the exotic animals in the first days of their occupation. Mak was devastated when confronted by a dusty, disreputable little park surrounding a small hill on which sat one of the holiest temples in Cambodia. His father attempted to cheer things up, but even he was dispirited to see the remembered glory of his youth destroyed and decrepit. It was cold, or at least as cold as Phnom Penh can get in the middle of winter, and just after lunch it began to rain. Before they headed back to the bus station, Mak's father bought him a brand-new jacket. Mak selected a bright orange puff-parka made in China. It was the most beautiful thing he'd ever owned, and so this disastrous trip to the city was redeemed somewhat.

But when they arrived home Mak's mother laid eyes on the parka and let out a cry. 'You foolish man,' she scolded his father. 'Why on earth would you buy the boy something the same colour as a monk's robes? He can't wear this—it is disrespectful and unlucky.' And so she folded up the parka and hid it away, and Mak never saw it again.

But this time Mak hoped things would turn out differently. His mother was happy and excited. Since his father's death she rarely wore her good sarongs, and he was pleased to see her looking so beautiful and felt proud of her. A slovenly *moto* drove up to them and said,

'Where are you going to, aunty?' She fished in her purse and pulled out the book, showing the driver the address on the cover. He squinted at it for some moments and finally handed it back to her. 'No good to me, sister, I can't read.' Embarrassed for him, and at her own insensitivity, his mother read him the address and the *moto* fluffed out his cheeks and said, 'Whoo, that's far. It's going to cost you.'

'Well, how much?' she asked, flustered now, and worried.

'Couple of dollars,' he said, looking saddened at the fact.

Mak's mother made a careful calculation in her head. She had brought exactly five dollars with her, and some of that had already gone on the truck trip, and they still had to get home. Phnom Penh had become much more expensive than she realised. 'Can you make it a dollar?' she pleaded. 'Take pity on an old widow.'

When they finally found the address, they discovered that it was not the glamorous office they had been expecting. It was, in fact, the author's humble villa in the suburbs. They knocked on the door and the great man himself answered. 'My son has written a novel,' said Mak's mother, handing the man the ratty exercise book. 'And it's good. We thought you might like to publish it.' The man was dumbfounded, and looked absently through the book.

'Is your son at university?' he asked.

'No, this is him here,' said Mak's mother proudly, pushing forward the skinny boy who looked a good deal younger than his fifteen years.

The great man laughed and said, 'But I can't publish a book written by some child.'

Mak's mother looked crestfallen. 'But it's good,' she said. 'As good as anything you've done, and I know,' she said, poking around in her ragged bag for the man's novels. 'Please, we heard you on the radio, sir. You are the only person we know who could make this happen.'

The author took pity on the dusty pair of peasants on his doorstep, and so invited them in. He gave them lunch, complete with fruit and coffee, and encouraged the boy's work, though he refused to even consider publishing it. 'Come back to me when you are at university,' he said, though he must have known that the idea of university was almost impossible to imagine for these two.

'Where else can we go, sir? I have spent so much money bringing my son to Phnom Penh today, I will never forgive myself if we don't try our best.'

'You could go to the Orussey Market,' the man said. 'Some of the booksellers there also publish. It's worth a try.'

As they left, the author handed Mak's mother a ten dollar note. 'Good luck, aunty—you are blessed with a wonderful son.' Mak and his mother stared aghast at the money.

At the Orussey Market they tramped around the book stalls. Most of the sellers shooed them away, but one woman, having a quiet period, took the manuscript from Mak and looked through it carefully. 'Are you sure you wrote this?' she asked.

'Yes,' said Mak, nervous.

'It's interesting. Leave it with me and I might be able to do something about it.'

Feeling defeated, Mak and his mother went to the bus station. 'Well, she seemed to like it, son,' said his mother, hopefully. But they heard nothing.

Two years later, Mak was in Phnom Penh, applying for university scholarships and looking for work. One day, at a big book shop in the city, he spied a book. Thinking the title looked familiar, he picked it up, and there on the cover was the author's name, 'Suong Mak'. His book had been published and he'd had no idea. He spent all the money he had buying three copies, and was so proud and happy he could barely contain himself. He had written many manuscripts since then, but because of his initial disappointment, he'd done nothing with them. Now there was proof that he had talent.

He went to the Orussey Market with a friend. Spotting the bookseller who had taken his manuscript, he sent his friend over to ask after his book—he felt far too shy to do it himself. 'Of course I have that book,' she told his friend, handing over a copy. 'It is one of my best sellers.' She looked at the friend carefully and then asked, 'Do you know the author?' When he said he did, the bookseller said, 'Tell him to come and see me. I have been trying to find him for years. I have some money for him.'

The day Mak returned alone to the bookseller's stall, she recognised him instantly. 'You silly little boy, where have you been? Your book has been a hit. Here, let me give you some money.' She took fifty dollars from her purse and handed it to him.

Mak walked away quickly, not quite certain he should believe his luck. He had never been given so much money in his life. Now he was an author.

KORAT

Needing to go on a visa run, I asked Panit if he wanted to come with me to Thailand to visit his brothers. I had no idea where these brothers actually lived in Thailand, but I thought it would be a great adventure. Panit simply couldn't refuse the opportunity to travel abroad and see his beloved siblings. After dozens of telephone calls were made, it was discovered that they all lived in a temple in Nakhon Ratchasima, the largest city in Thailand's northeast. The unwieldy name of the town was almost always shortened to a much simpler 'Korat'. And so we made our way there.

Panit's cousins and brothers in Korat kept up a fast-paced saffron-coloured whirl the whole time we stayed with them. They hired a driver and mini-van and these were a constant presence, ready at a moment's notice to take us to some suddenly remembered scenic point. It was seen as being of principal importance that I was kept constantly amused, and the monks were always admonishing Panit for not paying sufficient attention to my needs. Because of the conventions that forbade monks from pandering to the needs of worldly people, their hospitable instincts were thwarted at every turn, and poor Panit bore the brunt of their frustrations. 'A very lazy boy,' said one of his distant relatives who had also taken the robe in Thailand, as he watched me carting my own bag on my shoulder. 'He shames us. He should be carrying your bag at all times.'

Their new-found Thai prosperity had made Panit's relatives forget, too, the financial straits that Panit was accustomed to. When we visited a large shrine to the revered Thai monk Luang Pho Tho, Panit shyly asked if I might be able to buy him a cheap souvenir, a tiny plaster statue of the monk. His brothers, watching the whole interaction, chided him when I paid for the gift, quickly pulling out their own money, though that was also unseemly for a monk. When I said it was perfectly

OK, they gave me pained looks and said, 'It doesn't matter, it just looks bad. What will people say about him if they see you paying for everything he wants? It shames us as Cambodians.'

They all lived in a run-down but spacious old monastery next to the river. Panit's brother, a monk of long standing, had an unusual arrangement with a local woman. A plump, plain school teacher, she was slightly mannish and quite graceless, well past thirty, though she dressed in the most extraordinary clothes, cotton pyjamas with enormous Hello Kitty faces appliquéd at the breasts and frilly faux-skirts. This woman, I was told, was soon to become the monk's wife, once he had disrobed. Having been a monk for almost fifteen years, he felt his time in the religious life had come to an end, and, in anticipation of his resignation, had set about finding a suitable wife. She had to be Thai, because he planned never to live again in Cambodia. As much as I disapproved of her presence, she was rather sweet, and solicitous in the extreme, particularly when it came to providing food. All of her free time was taken up with caring for this monk and his brothers, in the understanding that he would soon become her husband.

I have been accustomed, all my life, to Mahayana monks who take on the vow of celibacy for a lifetime and who very rarely abandon their monastic vocations. The prevailing Theravada traditions of Thailand and Cambodia, however, were all based on the premise of temporary ordination, though that ordination might sometimes last for twenty years. But among Khmer monks I have never once met a man who is committed to the religious life for good. Every monk I knew had half an eye to the future, to wives, families and careers.

At night I stayed in a vast and strange hotel where I seemed to be the only guest. Though fancy and meant for great things, it was by now down at heel and the lobby was, I noticed with some satisfaction, flooded. For some reason I adore over-ambitious regional hotels that have been neglected. There is something so poignant about the marble lobbies, the dusty and unused ballrooms and conference facilities, the peeling carpets in the mirrored lifts. No-one was bothering to mop up the water in the lobby, and each time I came down the pool was a little deeper. My room was quite gigantic, the size of a small apartment, though the rate was very cheap. It had a certain kind of smell, one I associate with motel rooms in the 70s, and again I was comforted. This place smelled like home.

On our last day we went to the city shrine, dedi-cated to a woman who repelled the Laotian army in a murderous act of treachery. There were a number of *sala*, small open-sided gazebos, at the side of the shrine and in these women and elderly transsexuals were available to dance and sing as an offering to the city spirits. The dancing transsexuals, the *katoey*, were a fabulous and animated bunch I couldn't take my eyes off. Mostly they were tiny and shrivelled, with thickly applied make-up slowly melting off in the heat. There were one or two young *katoey* as well, learning the sacred dances, but once they were sure of our attention all of them started to goof around, giving me lascivious winks and moues and flirting with the handsome young monks. But I was impressed by their sacred purpose, and the reverence and respect with which they were treated by the townspeople. They were at the very heart of the city's spiritual life, and they served an essential purpose.

The monks insisted that lots and lots of pictures were taken. I had by now learned that this was one of the main purposes of all outings, to be meticulously recorded and photographed, though in a digital age the images are never printed—remaining trapped on dozens and dozens of full memory cards. After the city shrine, we took a long drive to a rural temple where there is an ancient Khmer reclining Buddha kept in a semi-ruined state but in a nice modern *sala*. Quite a few Thai people were there, offering incense and lotus flowers. But the Cambodian monks were here for quite a different reason. 'This is a Khmer Buddha,' they whispered to me triumphantly. 'All of this is Khmer land, stolen by the Thais. Some day soon it will return to us. It is destiny.'

We strolled all over the complex, the Thais staring with fascination as the monks all spoke to each other in

Khmer. We came to a colourful and elaborately decorated building that was much praised by all, and everyone took turns having their photographs taken on its steps. After a few minutes a Thai man appeared and spoke in a panicked fashion to Panit's older brother, gesturing at the beautiful building. The monk blanched and, turning to us, he said, 'This is a terrible place—it is a crematorium oven.' When he said it in Khmer the other monks all shrieked and ran from the spot. The older brother fixed me with a smile and explained cheerily, 'Very bad luck—maybe we will die tomorrow.'

The unfortunate photo taking outside the crematorium had spooked Panit, and for the rest of the day he was moody and difficult. A stickler for tradition and respectful of magic at the best of times, he now grew almost compulsive, and the day became an extended observation of bowings, prayings and frantic mutterings of mantras. No shrine was left unworshipped, and there are plenty of shrines in northeastern Thailand. This suited me fine, for the most part, as one of my principal interests is the practice of folk religion, and it is normally me frustrating everyone else with my insistence on studying each and every spiritual monument we encounter.

We drove to a restaurant that was situated in a transformed farm, the kind of place where you paid a steep entry fee in order to be able to enjoy the equally steep prices of all the facilities inside. The monks were all delirious with excitement, though I was quietly fuming. It was exactly the sort of place I wouldn't visit in a million years. Inside were all kinds of kitschy restaurants and food concessions developed around a theme, and shops that sold miniature milk carts full of flowers and novelty vases in the shape of frogs.

We eventually settled for lunch at a recreated Northern Thai farmhouse overlooking an artificial lake, and a truly delicious meal came forth, a banquet of fiery northeastern Thai standards like green papaya salad, spicy minced chicken and lumps of sticky rice. As convention dictated, the monks sat together at an elevated table eating and talking, while the three worldly people hunched over a nearby coffee table. This didn't stop the monks from involving us in their conversation. The meal had renewed their interest in sightseeing, and plans were being made for well into the afternoon, and perhaps even the evening. This made me nervous, because I had a very expensive hotel room booked and paid for in Bangkok, and there was no way I was giving that up for another night in my flooded and deserted hotel in Korat. I had to put my foot down.

'We really need to leave at about two,' I explained, 'three at the latest. I have commitments in Bangkok.' This had been the plan always, enunciated since the hour we had first arrived in Korat. But the monks set to murmuring, and Panit's oldest brother stood up from the table and came to address me.

'But this is an impossible plan, unreasonable. There is still so much you need to see.' The other monks all nodded in agreement, many of them wearing shocked and offended expressions. I knew this tactic well—it was the one always adopted when you tried to stick to a plan after a monk had changed his mind. And I also knew that, unless I was prepared to be an absolute arsehole, I would never leave northeastern Thailand.

'Nonetheless,' I intoned solemnly, in my best grumpy old man voice, 'it is a plan I need to follow. It hasn't changed, and you have known about it for two days.' There was a hurried conference in Khmer among the monks and Panit, and then in Thai with the lady schoolteacher. And then a pointed silence. I was clearly in the doghouse. But then, as we all filed back in to the pleasure garden, all was forgiven.

As our time together was due to end very soon, there was a frenzy of photo taking.

One by one, the monks came up to have their photograph taken with me perched perilously, if not coquettishly, on the curved arm of a throne set in a mock Chinese temple. As each monk left, he presented me with a gift, a small amulet of the type beloved by Thais, tiny bronze images of Buddhas or monks encased in a clear plastic cover. Proceeding from novice to most senior, the amulets became increasingly large and decorative. When one of Panit's tattooed cousins finally got to me, he scooped the others by presenting me with a heavy and lavish talisman, easily the size of my hand and, I imagined, quite impossible to wear around one's neck. Everyone cooed at its opulence. This cousin had been my great pal while I was in Korat, and could be quickly and easily distinguished from the other identically dressed monks by the heavy tattooing that covered both arms and all the visible skin up to his neck.

Getting wind of what was happening, Panit's older brother, the most senior monastic present, began fishing in his orange satchel and, triumphantly, drew from it an even more elaborate devotional item, this one the size of a laptop and weighing at least a kilo. 'Something for you to remember me by,' he said, pushing it into my hands and casting a competitive look at the tattooed young monk, who stood dejected in another corner. Now everyone was clapping and laughing, delighted that the younger man's effort at impressing had been defeated. I, however, always favour the underdog, and so it was the smaller amulet that found pride of place on my little shrine when I got back to Phnom Penh.

THE ANGKOR PRINCESS

Shamans are common in Cambodia, and people often turn to them in moments of desperation and great need. The Cambodian people are convinced of the presence of spirits in this world and of the possibility of communicating with them and the importance of keeping them happy. In small towns and villages shamans are ubiquitous, and often the first point of call when people become ill or find themselves in troubling situations. Often women, these shamans are community leaders, though their power seems to carry with it a slight creepiness—they are sometimes feared more than respected. The powers of a shaman also carry with them the possibility of self-destruction.

I was quite desperate to visit a shaman, but all of my efforts came to nothing. Everyone had one they'd consulted and promised to introduce me, but when the time came the shamans always pulled out. Foreigners, they said, interfered with their patron spirit. I wasn't surprised, because I had encountered this exact problem in Vietnam—most psychics, channels and shamans incorporated elements of nationalism in their sayings, and indeed many of the spirit figures they communicated with were national heroes, generals and warriors who had expelled foreigners. Apparently even on the other side they didn't look kindly on outsiders. The extraordinary persistence of spirit worship in South-East Asia has been attributed by academics to this very source, 'a way of making sense of the unsettling effects of the penetration and transformation of local worlds by new political and economic relations', according to Philip Taylor.

But my friend Chanphal, the successful young songwriter and novelist, managed to come through. His favourite shaman, a woman he visited regularly and viewed as his principal spiritual advisor, was more than happy to see me. 'It's because she is real,' he said. 'She has nothing to fear from you. But don't be expecting theatrics. Hers is a very simple ceremony—she simply dons a scarf and offers some incense and goes into a trance. There is no drinking whiskey, smoking cigars or dancing. The spirit she channels is an educated person, and so offers only calm and rational advice.'

So one cool morning we took a tuk tuk to a farm about forty-five minutes outside of Phnom Penh. Suong Mak came with us, bringing with him an utterly disdainful attitude. 'This stuff drives me crazy,' he muttered, his slender form crumpled into the corner of the tuk tuk. 'Why do Cambodian people believe this nonsense? I'm only coming to see what fools you are willing to make of yourselves. It will be great for a book.'

We arrived at a tidy and exceedingly prosperous looking farm. The houses were of two storeys and made of brick, unlike the neighbouring farmhouses, which were small wooden structures on stilts. The shaman rushed out to greet us, accompanied by two sturdy-looking young men who were shirtless and dressed only in *krama*. Seeing our strange and slightly glamorous group arrive, they quickly ran into one of the houses and got properly dressed.

The shaman was a small and plainly dressed farm woman with dark skin and a lined face. Knowing the toll that hard farm work takes on people in Cambodia, I rightly guessed her to be in her early forties, though she looked ten years older. She was pleasant and shy and totally unassuming, and I felt instantly at ease in her presence. She said she was privileged to have me visit, and she asked after the cost of the tuk tuk. When we told her she looked pleased and said, 'Oh, you were thoroughly cheated. I pay a quarter of that.' People were always happy to hear I'd been ripped off.

We were seated in the front room of the most opulent house. Chanphal told me that one of the shaman's followers had become a rich and successful businessman because of her advice and guidance, and so had paid for her new house. The two young men re-emerged in crisp clean T-shirts and smart trousers. One of them, the shaman's son-in-law, was sent on a number of errands, serving us tea and fetching a pile of Chanphal's books, which for some reason had to be present during the ceremony. The shaman's son was made to sit next to me. 'He has just finished university and is fluent in English,' said the shaman. 'But he can't find a job yet.' So he translated for me through the whole ceremony.

This son had been instrumental in a new phase of the shaman's development. He had recently had a dream in which a *Naga*, a serpent spirit, had appeared to him. But this *Naga* had feet and could speak, and he had told him that his mother was a great spiritual power who would change the world. He had told his mother this dream, and for the next few nights she was plagued with headaches and insomnia until, finally, the *Naga* came to her in a vision and told her he was ready to speak. This momentous occasion was yet to occur, but was scheduled for the next *Uposatha*, the Buddhist Sabbath of the full moon.

But for today we had to make do with her usual supernatural guide, a princess who had lived in the times of Angkor. The shaman put on a white lace scarf of the kind Cambodian women wear to temple and she lit a stick of incense and suddenly she was, without ceremony, possessed. The princess had a high pitched voice and liked to sing songs. She asked me if I enjoyed her songs, and I was unnerved by the strange conversation I was forced to have with her in front of all of the observers. I dared not glance at Mak, who was scribbling notes furiously in his journal. Chanphal scolded him for this, saying it would break the magic, but he wrote on determinedly.

Apparently the princess, unlike the farm woman, was fluent in English, Chinese and French. 'But I notice she kept on at you in Khmer,' said Mak later. I was desperate for practical advice—how do I become a better person; what must I do to improve my career; how do I write a bestseller? But the princess was maddeningly enigmatic, answering in lofty generalisations and straying frequently into rhapsodic praise for the Cambodian people and nation. The Angkorean princess was something of a propagandist. A second stick of incense was lit, and the princess was presented with a can of winter melon drink, which she declared delicious, though strange. We also slid over a basket of gifts which we had earlier purchased for her: lotus flowers, coconuts, fruit and a bottle of cheap perfume. In among the gifts was a discreet envelope of cash, which the princess quietly slid into her blouse.

Suong Mak, unable to contain himself any longer, shuffled forth on his knees and began to pepper the princess with questions, the answers to which he carefully wrote down. Occasionally he openly laughed, and once he turned to me and said loudly in English, 'Oh my God, all of these answers are wrong. What silliness.' The princess began to look worried and finally, in an effort to stop Mak's questions, asked us if we wanted another song. We said a relieved yes. Despite my doubts,

I felt strongly protective of the princess and didn't want the poor shaman to lose face.

Proceedings began to slow somewhat when the princess began a long diatribe about Cambodian politics and ASEAN, and even Chanphal grew restless and turned to the son-in-law and began to chat. Cambodians have an unsettling habit of starting up side conversations if they are bored with what they are hearing, no matter what the place or context. Finally we were reined in by another song and an appeal for extra funds, only if we were inspired to give them, of course. The princess said money was needed for the introduction to her celestial friend the *Naga* spirit who would be appearing in a week or two. I handed over another ten dollars and Chanphal gave her a wad of riel, but Mak sat there in stark and unmoving disapproval.

Leaving her trance, the shaman slumped forward and tore the white scarf from around her plump neck. The son-in-law rushed forth with a small cup of tea, and Chanphal explained to me, 'She is exhausted, you see, after her work. It tires her body to do this. But she does it because she loves us.'

Smiling weakly at me, the shaman said, 'You are one of us now, sir. I hope you will come to see the *Naga*.'

As we were leaving the shaman called to me again from her front room, quietly and humbly. I was worried she would want more money, but instead she said to me, 'Please, sir—my son has no work and he has finished university. You can see how well he speaks English. Can't you find him a job?' I was in no position to find anyone any kind of job, but I lied and said that yes, I would ask around. I felt horrible that I couldn't help. The son just smiled at me, embarrassed too at the slight desperation of his mother's request. I wished him luck.

In the tuk tuk home, Mak gave us a cutting run-down of the shaman's failings. The princess, apparently, had given wrong dates and times for her historical era. She used words clumsily, often employing the wrong word in an effort to sound grandiose. And she was very, very shaky in her understanding of the ASEAN treaties. 'What do you expect,' I said in exasperation. 'She lived in the twelfth century!'

BULL'S PENIS

'Once, it took me four years to pay back a loan of ten dollars,' said Mak during a hot, lazy afternoon when there was nothing to do but watch Indian soap operas on TV. Mak became loquacious on such occasions, his novelist's mind springing into action and telling me all kinds of sad and touching stories. All of my friends in Phnom Penh lived according to a complex series of debts and loans. Mak told me about all the disastrous times he had borrowed money from friends—small amounts that nonetheless took years to repay. Though in his mouth the stories were sweet and funny and pointed to the generosity of the lenders, I couldn't help but feel sad and even guilty about how lives could be made stressful, friendships and even families destroyed, over such piddling amounts. I found it difficult to get upset over the waste or loss of even fifty or sixty dollars, amounts that could still change lives in Cambodia.

Not for the first time, I was struck by the fact that one of the measures of poverty is the preoccupation with small circumstances. In my privileged life, everyone, even the most decorously struggling, was concerned with a much wider-spanning arc of existence. Futures, careers, relationships, homes—these were all the serious concerns of the day. In Cambodia, people fretted about meals, items of clothing, visits to the doctor, buying petrol. These immediate concerns were actual and acute problems that always needed solving.

And of course, the Cambodians are just as concerned about marriages and jobs and old age and all of the other big things. It's just that a focus on these is often and necessarily crowded out by worry for the present day concerns. But there was another side to this: a pleasure in and care about the small things. When people cooked for me they took an inordinate amount of care in how the food was presented, how the bowls were arranged on the tray that was brought to me, the colours of curry and dipping sauce.

I struggle in discussing this because I despise the glamourisation of poverty that is so often a part of travel to places like Cambodia. We are all of us guilty of romanticising squalor and imagining that a simpler life must be happier and more content than our own. It is simply not true when the measure of that simplicity is no access to medicine, education or clean food and water. When children die of diarrhoea or malnutrition, as they regularly do in rural Cambodia, it is immoral to suggest that somehow their families lead a more blissful and natural existence, free of our complex concerns.

But the human spirit inclines towards happiness, and seeks beauty and leisure wherever it is. You only need to read one or two of the memoirs about the Pol Pot years to realise that, in the face of the most tremendous horror and oppression, people were still managing to laugh, have children and find some kind of meaning in their existence. The whole nation of Cambodia stands as evidence to the fact of resilience. And there is no denying the subtle charms of lives lived with a careful attention to the present and the everyday.

While I was in Cambodia I was certainly receiving an education in the importance of little things. But perhaps it was simply a confirmation of a pre-existing prejudice, a strongly and long-held belief that when I travel it is the little things that give me the most pleasure and the greatest memories. I am often bored by the grand: the great sight, the spectacle. Nothing bores me as much as a parade, and I am quite allergic to festivals of any form. I would much rather spend a dull afternoon in a friend's living room watching local soap operas. There is a subtle aesthetic at work in this preference, and I dare say a great deal of snobbery, but I cannot deny my feelings.

One of my greatest convictions is that the traveller should instantly establish roots in a new temporary residence. This can be done quickly through frequenting regularly a local cafe, restaurant or bar. After three consecutive visits your repeated presence will be noticed, and by the fifth visit you will be family. And so it was at my friend Heng's restaurant. Whenever I turned up there in the capacity of customer he treated me with a brisk professionalism, rarely betraying our strange intimacy, though my table was served more quickly and with greater warmth than any other. I liked to sit upstairs, where a rotating cast of singers sang Khmer favourites to a mostly unlistening audience. I was reliably informed that the performers were in fact the cream of Cambodian singers, forced to take lowly gigs like these to make money in a tough market. Heng would often ask me if I wanted to sing, assuring me that the resident musicians were possessed of a full catalogue of English favourites. '"Hotel California"?' he would suggest, hopefully. But I managed to stay in my seat.

One night I brought a table full of friends and Heng came over, casting a stern eye over the gathering. I knew that in a night or two I would be subjected to a late-night assessment of all of their shortcomings. As a matter of principle, Heng hated any other Cambodians I was associated with. Though both of us were convinced that our charade of distance was perfectly played, halfway through the night one of my friends leaned over and asked me suspiciously, 'Do you know that waiter?'

When the menus were handed out, Panit took a quick look and exclaimed, with absolute pleasure, 'Look, they have bull penis soup!' We all flicked through the hefty menu, which featured full offerings from four different cuisines: Chinese, Khmer, Thai and Vietnamese, all reproduced in unappetisingly yellow-ish photographs. And there at the bottom of page sixteen sat the promised bull penis soup, an unassuming little bowl of brown broth in a small iron pot, with no recognisable lumps. Naturally several of us ordered it. I have inherited an incapacity to resist the most repulsive item on the menu. My mother, a great consumer of cookbooks, is famous for scouring each new book for the most distinctly horrible recipe and then whipping it up for the family: 'Tripe fried in beer with pineapple and pumpkin—why, that sounds like the perfect dinner.'

As we chatted and drank our mysterious 'cocktails' (the only description offered in the menu), various dishes came out, but after half an hour or so there was still no sign of the much-anticipated bull penis. Someone called Heng over and demanded to know what had happened to our soup.

Cultivating the right mix of frostiness and deference, he assured us that it was indeed bubbling on the stove. 'It takes a long time to cook penis,' he explained, shooting me a withering look. I knew my friends had been judged and found wanting. Finally, at the end of almost an hour, the little pots of soup arrived, still steaming.

I had imagined a long, eel-like object curled up in the broth, and was disappointed to discover instead a few gristly, flower-like lumps lurking in the liquid: obviously the penis had been cut into sections. Heng watched on in delight as the men sat and considered their meal. A quietness had descended upon our previously noisy group. The penis had been boiled in a broth containing medicinal Chinese herbs, and the unmistakeable smell wafted up into our faces. I was the first to eat a piece, and once in my mouth it was deeply unpleasant, chewy and slimy like a piece of tendon. The only taste was the medicinal soup. One by one my friends began theirs, and all pleasure drained from their faces. What had seemed like a fun idea an hour ago now became an unwanted obligation. Swallowing his first chunk of penis, Panit looked up at me and said, 'I feel some disgust.'

Once I had dutifully finished my whole bowl, one of the group who had resisted the temptation asked me, 'How did it taste?'

'Well, soft and chewy, rubbery and almost entirely flavourless. Exactly like you'd expect a penis to taste,' I said.

'And you'd know,' murmured Heng as he leaned in and began to collect the bowls.

KHMER NEW YEAR

Battambang is built around the banks of the Sangke River. The second-biggest city in Cambodia, it is charming and sleepy, its people phlegmatic and softly spoken. As you approach the city you are confronted by a huge and terrifying black-skinned god, the founder and protector of Battambang, a deity taken very seriously by all who live there. From early morning people arrive at the base of the statue to pray and make offerings of roast chicken, whiskey, flowers and fruit. Anyone leaving Battambang, especially to seek their fortune in Phnom Penh, must first pay a visit to their fearsome black grandfather and beg his permission to leave.

The construction of the statue is surrounded with myths and terrifying tales constantly repeated by the people of Battambang. The present statue is, it must be said, very fine. Monolithic in proportions, it is beautifully executed and well-proportioned, a claim that can't be made for all public sculpture in Cambodia. The demon's tremendous black limbs are strong and powerful, depicted as he is, squatting in a strangely masculine way, his arms held out before him clutching a baton and an offering bowl. The demon is said to have used the baton to claim the land around Battambang, and though the locals swear to his being an exclusive protector, similar myths and deities are to be found in Laos and Thailand.

Nonetheless, Ta Dambang, as the black grandfather is known, is treated very seriously by the residents of Battambang, and among the more superstitious, is even feared. It is said that the original sculptor hired to create the new statue (the first, antique, one was much smaller) had carved a delicately refined man with a sweet and gentle face. When the prototype was unveiled there were hoots of protest and the next morning the artist was found dead, beaten in his bed. Ta Dambang, the people whispered, had appeared in the night, furious that the man had tried to present him as such an effete. So then a new, doubtless worried, artist had to be found, and this one had done all in his power to make the being appear terrifying in every aspect. And while people in Battambang keep small photographs of the statue in their houses and cars, it is rare to see miniature replicas. When I asked Panit if we could buy one he looked at me like I was crazy. 'Never—who would dare to create such a thing? Don't play with fire, brother.'

I had decided to spend Khmer New Year in Battambang. Almost everyone I knew had fled Phnom Penh to be in their ancestral homeland and the city was something of a ghost town. I was told that the buses would all be filled days in advance and that tickets were at a premium but, choosing to travel on the day itself, I discovered the buses almost deserted. The tickets, however, were all monstrously inflated, and I payed almost three times the usual fare to get to Battambang.

The bus driver played DVDs of Korean pop music for the whole five-hour drive, probably because there was hardly anyone on the bus and no-one seemed to care. In truth, he actually played only two DVDs of Korean pop, the same two, over and over again, obviously favourites of the young conductor who would often reach over to repeat Big Bang's 'Fantastic Baby'.

In the evening of the New Year all Cambodian families conduct a ceremony welcoming the new angel of the year. Each year has a protective angel, following a seven-year cycle. My friend Kakkada had hoped I would be with his family in Battambang to celebrate it, but when the appointed time came, I was still on the bus as it made its slow, endlessly stopping progress. After that point he rang me every half-hour demanding to know where I was. If I had no idea, he asked me to describe the landscape and any distinctive landmarks. This would always be met with a grumpy sigh. 'You are still so far way,' he complained. 'Why didn't you leave Phnom Penh earlier?'

Battambang seemed like such a lovely town on the quiet New Year's night. It's almost the perfect size, and approaching the colonial city past the outstretched arms and terrifying face of the great black god creates its own special frisson. For me it is the most charming place in Cambodia, the sort of place I could imagine living. Even late at night there were people worshipping at the base of the Battambang god, who was dramatically spotlighted to further increase his spectacular presence.

Getting off the bus in Battambang I was almost bowled over by the heat. The Khmer New Year represents the very pinnacle of the hot season, and it is little wonder that the principal amusement of the holiday is soaking other people with water in public. In preparation for this, streetside vendors were selling little see-through plastic wallets to put your mobile phone in. I sat at the bus station alone with my single, small bag. The circling *motoduhps* called out to me and scoffed when I said I was waiting for a friend. 'Tonight, no friend,' they taunted. 'Cambodian New Year! Nobody is coming for you.' And after a half-hour I began to believe they were right. Kakkada had been calling me every twenty minutes while I was on the bus, but now that I had actually arrived he was nowhere to be seen. Not for the first time, I was moderately perplexed by Cambodian notions of hospitality. At last, after more than forty-five minutes, Kakkada veered up the dark, deserted street on his motorcycle. He was quite drunk, and apologetic.

'My friends wouldn't let me leave,' he explained. 'They kept making me drink.' I said nothing but climbed up behind him, preparing to die. Fortunately there was not a single other bike on the road. Everyone else in Battambang was at home with their families. There was a single restaurant open, a backpacker joint where a dwarf served us noodles and banana fruit shakes and brought more beer for Kakkada, despite my protests. Because Battambang is really just a small town, Kakkada knew the dwarf and everyone else at the restaurant.

He had found me a hotel by the river, right next door to a wat, and late at night it seemed a picturesque location. Because we arrived late, the hotel staff were already settled in for the night on fold-out beds or mats thrown onto the gleaming lobby floor. The women were in floral pyjamas while the men wore tight black singlets and baggy shorts. They were pleasant enough about our interruption, though.

From my window all I could see were the upturned golden eaves of the temple roof. But the next morning at 4.30 a.m.—exactly—the temple turned on its PA system, and a mix of Buddhist chant and Khmer dance music came flooding in. It was obvious that I was going to be getting some early starts.

At New Year everyone was at their religious best, and soon people were flooding into the temple to attend the special morning prayers and Dharma talk. I decided to join them, and sat with the elderly women and men on the cool tile floor of the teaching hall. I was always surprised by how much Pali Cambodian lay people seemed to know by heart. Even women had whole swathes memorised, though they spent no time living in a monastery, as most men do.

Soon Kakkada arrived, with his entire family, all brothers. They shared something of the same look, and Kakkada insisted I go through them, one by one, and point out the key differences in each, within their hearing. At the end of this ritual Kakkada told me proudly, 'See, I am the most handsome in the family. Everyone says so. None of my brothers can compete.' At this the other five nodded in resigned agreement.

Three days after the Khmer New Year I was back in Phnom Penh and went to Monument Books for breakfast. Inside this elegant and truly excellent English-language bookshop there is not only a toy store but a branch of the Blue Pumpkin, a wildly popular bakery and cafe. But on this day the Blue Pumpkin had run out of food, and the staff was entirely unfussed at this extraordinary state of affairs. Clearly it was the Khmer New Year and no-one was serving food—why should they? No words could express my immense frustration at learning this almost impossible-to-believe fact. I had come for my blue cheese sandwich and instead I was faced with the choice of a two-day-old chocolate croissant or a lime slushie, hardly food to soothe a savage beast. But argument or even complaint was futile. The New Year is a time of endurance cloaked as a celebration—I imagine it was what Christmas must once have been like in the West before the advent of seven-day shopping.

And so I sat with my laptop in the almost deserted cafe and sipped sourly at a Coke, feeling the destruction it wreaked on my utterly empty stomach. Generally I liked being at Monument Books, it was quiet, as a bookshop should be, and as all places that cater almost exclusively to foreigners tend to be in Cambodia. The attendants would chat, gathered in small tight circles at some corner, but apart from them there was nothing but the occasional clatter of glasses being washed in a distant hidden kitchen.

Until a truly enormous American woman in late middle age arrived. I saw her hair ascend the stairs long before I caught sight of any other part of her anatomy. She was possessed of a tall beehive of the singular fashion normally only seen on drag queens or women belonging to breakaway Mormon cults. Her plentiful form was covered in a loose and flowing floral muumuu, the type of which I hadn't seen in about thirty years. On one side of her was a short but plump husband, bespectacled and pink-faced. And on the other was a demure Cambodian girl roughly the size of one of the American woman's arms.

After they took the table immediately next to mine in the entirely empty restaurant, the hard-faced, acne-scarred waiter ran to their group and informed them that there was no food to be had. 'Bob, they've got no food!' shouted the woman in a voice that indicated that Bob was quite deaf. Bob smiled sagely as the woman flipped through the menu in a panic. 'Well, what have you got for us, honey?' she demanded of the waiter.

'Coke float,' he suggested.

'Bob! They've only got Coke floats!' she cried in a mixture of alarm and pleasure. 'Well, that'll have to do,' she said with good cheer. 'Three Coke floats!'

It soon become clear that Bob and his bouffanted lady were missionaries, something I had guessed at one glance. Wholesome, elderly Americans in the company of young Cambodians are almost always missionaries. Indeed, missionaries are pretty thick on the ground in Cambodia, though they meet with rare success. Filmmaker and old Cambodia hand James Gerrand told me of seeing missionaries in even the most remote corners of Cambodia. In Rattanakiri, a tribal area in the northeast of Cambodia on the border of Laos, indefatigable Christian missionaries have managed to make their bothersome presence felt, in open hostility to the deeply held animistic beliefs of the Hill Tribe people. Tensions are created in communities when some family groups convert to Christianity, leaving those who stand by their traditional worldview feeling besieged, threatened and often patronised.

But it seems sometimes as though there are more missionaries than converts, and those who do convert seem to be there more for the free English classes (a popular ruse for religious professionals), free medical care and, in some cases, free accommodation. A tuk tuk driver I knew was an enthusiastic Baptist because, having been injured in a traffic accident, a Christian mission was the only place that would provide him with free medical care. After a few weeks in their small clinic, having grasped the extent of the freebies on offer, including free education for his two children, he was more than willing to sign up for the whole deal. These days he teaches Sunday school and his tuk tuk is adorned with a small cross. 'You might know my pastor, David,' he said to me. 'He's from Australia too.'

The Mrs Reverend Bob was here to match make, it seemed, though the young woman was clearly uninterested in the boy they had selected as a partner. 'Hor is such a lovely boy,' said the woman. 'So handsome and kind, and a good Christian too. One of the most reliable boys we have at church. And I know he's got a soft spot for you, honey. So we thought we'd maybe organise something for the two of you to get to know each other better.'

The young woman, bespectacled and earnest, said quietly, 'Hor has no money.'

'Money!' shrieked the American woman. 'It's not about money. It's about love. Hor is a good-looking boy, and there's nothing he wouldn't do for us. We'd trust him with our life—wouldn't we, Bob?' Bob nodded demurely.

As the Coke floats arrived the young woman, clearly uncomfortable, shifted her attention to Bob. 'But pastor, you must understand. I can't marry someone with no money. What would be the point? It's not appropriate, for him or for me. I have my mother to think about, and my future. Hor is not educated and he just works at the church. It is unsuitable.'

This only goaded the pastor's wife who, taking a substantial sip of her Coke float for sustenance, mounted her defence. 'Oh honey, this isn't the way to think. Money, jobs—these aren't the things that a marriage is about! It's about two people who love each other, who care for each other and love God and want to have beautiful children. Why, the pastor had no money at all when I met him. But he sure was good-looking,' she said, breaking into a quivering, multi-chinned giggle. It seemed impossible to imagine that Pastor Bob was ever good-looking, but there is no accounting for the myth-making potential of memory.

Almost on cue a bashful and beautiful young man came up the stairway. He had taken a great deal of care over his appearance. He made his way meekly over to the Christian table and smiled at the pastor and his wife, avoiding the glance of the serious young woman. It was almost exactly the wrong time for him to appear, and the young woman's cheeks were flushed with embarrassment and possibly anger.

'Why, Hor, honey,' said the pastor's wife as he sat down noiselessly next to her, and she drew him into her ample embrace. Almost entirely engulfed by fat and floral fabric, Hor let out a muffled giggle. Another round of Coke floats was ordered, but I could see the young woman fidgeting and looking around her, avoiding eye contact with the luckless Hor.

'I'm so sorry,' she said, standing with her handbag at her side and fishing for her motorcycle keys. 'But I cannot stay. Cambodian New Year, so much to do for my family.'

'But baby, we just ordered you another Coke,' said Rev. Mrs, herself mortified by how it was all panning out. The young woman wavered for a moment, her manners getting the better of her. But just as she was about to sit down again, she glanced at Hor, whose eyes were staring solidly at some point on the table in front of him, and said, 'No, really. I must go. My mother expects me.' In a cloud of perfume, she strolled away from the table, her high heels clattering across the wooden floors. Hor looked at her in complete desolation as she descended the stairs.

WAYS OF HELPING

When he came to meet me at the Saigon 2007 cafe, Kimly had casually brought out a phone and charger from his bag, and plugged them in to the power outlet on the wall right near us. It was an exceedingly warm day, and though each table had its own individual wall-mounted fan blowing on it, ours was disabled due to Kimly's charging phone. So as we sat and read and chatted, I grew increasingly hot and uncomfortable, mopping at my brow with a handkerchief. After some time the cafe owner came out with a glass of iced water. She pulled Kimly's charger from the wall and plugged the fan back in, directing it straight at my face. Then she turned to Kimly and began to yell at him in Khmer. When she walked away, I asked Kimly what she had said. 'She scolded me for not taking care of you properly,' he said. 'She also said how beautiful you were. You are lucky, with your fat face. Cambodians love this—a full face is a beautiful face.' I had in fact been struck by the chubbiness of the popular young singers and actors I had seen on TV and in video clips. And I sensed, also, what Kimly meant by beauty. No-one for a moment imagined that these fleshy celebrities were sexy or seductive. But their pale plump pleasantness, those same qualities I possessed, were representative of good luck and good cheer.

Suddenly struck by an idea, Kimly asked if he could use my pen and a page from my journal. Sliding them over to him, he proceeded to carefully draw a compass. 'Phnom Penh,' he said to me with the air of someone letting me in on a great secret, 'has a north, south, east and west. We can go in any direction you like!' He looked at me in a pleased fashion, and with great expectancy. I was perplexed, though, because he had got north and south confused. Was it a mix up with English, or was he really so unsure of the cardinal points? The more I travelled with Kimly the more I realised that, despite his intimate topographical knowledge of his own small section of Phnom Penh, he had almost no idea where anything else was. Like every tuk tuk and *mohto* driver, he had no idea of street names, or the names of any of Phnom Penh's principal landmarks.

Because of his bravado and his usually excellent English, it was easy for me to forget the utter desperation of his life and his past. He was a lonely orphan living in absolute poverty in a hall in a Buddhist monastery. In recent days he told me of the mental warfare he was engaged in with the monk whose room he lived outside of. The monk was given food every day by lay people, food far surplus to his actual needs. So Kimly's main source of nutrition was the extra packets of instant noodles that the faithful gave to the monk. These would be passed on to the temple boys, but in recent weeks the monk had become stingy with his gifts, holding a grudge against Kimly for some reason. 'He wants me to beg him for his noodles, but I won't do it,' he said, shaking his head stubbornly. This proud position meant that on some days he was close to starving, and I had noticed that his already skinny frame had shrunk in the past couple of weeks. But Kimly's personal code of conduct meant that he would starve rather than beg from a greedy and petty-minded monk. I realised I had no idea what his life must really be like, what it must be like to rely on free packets of noodles to survive.

My affection for the man, and his clearly noble and independent spirit, meant that I always felt inclined to help him, but he became shy and even angry when faced with charitable acts. I experimented with ways of helping, and found that gifts of money discreetly slipped into a safe section of his ever-present backpack went unmentioned, and so he obviously felt this was a sufficiently dignified process. One day, however, I overstepped the mark. Kimly had been exceptionally kind to me and had gone out of his way to take me to a distant monastery filled with unique statuary. It was a dilapidated and dusty place with an attached funeral home, just like some of the big temples I had visited in Bangkok. While we were there the chanting was going on non-stop and the flags were all at half-mast. 'The abbott has just died,' said Kimly, after drilling a nearby monk.

Inside one of the buildings in the complex was a huge gathering of people, both monks and lay people, and it was packed with floral tributes and huge blow-ups of the recently departed abbott. The man himself was in the centre of it all, in a glass-topped refrigerated coffin. Naturally, everyone insisted I go and look at him, though, like most Westerners, I have almost no experience at the viewing of dead bodies, and find it hard to cope with the required etiquette. We joined a queue of people waiting to file past the coffin, and I paid careful attention to their actions so that I could emulate them perfectly. Take off hat and glasses, hold hands in prayer position, walk past the coffin, peer in and, before leaving the hall, swing back round in front of the coffin to get on your knees and bow. I was terrified I would do something wrong, but in the end everyone seemed pleased with my performance, and Kimly was beaming with pride.

We then toured the Buddhist fun park, half finished and dangerous, and then swung home via a Chinese cult housed in a palatial Chinese-style temple with an immense statue of the fat Buddha of the future sitting out front. Kimly insisted we go inside, where the young Khmer women who were converts fussed around us and made us observe all of the strange little rituals of the group. They insisted, for example, that as men we must take the right-side stairway to the main shrine, a requirement I remember used to be enforced at Buddhist temples in Vietnam, but which had largely disappeared. Once in the clean, spacious prayer hall with its surprisingly demure shrine to the Buddha of the future, something—a mysterious mystical force, or heat exhaustion and a sunburn?—forced me down on to my knees to pray.

One of the girls fetched the master, and I sat waiting in true fear, expecting some kind of robust, Moonie-like character who would assail me with doctrine. Instead, a mild-mannered little Taiwanese man of early middle age shuffled out in cheap slacks, flip-flops and a terrible haircut. He seemed perplexed to find himself here, in this mammoth and largely unvisited complex that the surrounding Cambodians avoid because they find it spooky. 'Not many people at all come,' he admitted with charming humility. 'I was sent here, and I do my best. They are very sweet people you know. You seem like a nice man. Why don't you join us?' This kind of offhanded proselytisation was almost effective, as I considered whiling away my twilight years in air-conditioned comfort ministering to a tiny and largely confused congregation.

The sweet cult leader offered us lunch, but Kimly recoiled at the mention of vegetarianism, and insisted that we were OK. We drove quickly to a nearby restaurant that, comfortingly, served meat. 'That was a strange place,' said Kimly, shaking his head. 'I would never go there alone. Why are they even in Cambodia?

And all those girls. Strange.' To get the cult out of his head, Kimly over-ordered a thoroughly delicious lunch, compensating for his brush with the occult by getting only meat dishes and two huge bottles of beer. He introduced me to *char k'dao*, a Cambodian favourite of chicken fried with lemongrass, chilli and basil, and almost the perfect dish to be served in such a climate. We were served by a statuesque and really very beautiful transsexual who all the young staff called *Look Srey*, the honorific for an older woman of high status.

I noticed, not for the first time, that Kimly was possessed of no table manners at all. The basic Cambodian conventions—serving the oldest person first and waiting for them to start eating—seemed unknown to him, and he chatted animatedly while he piled his plate high and tucked right in. I felt slightly offended, despite myself. I had become used to the formal hierarchies of Khmer society, where I came right up near the top. I saw his casual manner as a slight, though in truth it reflected nothing but his institutionalised upbringing, where the finer points of social grace were not imparted.

Kimly was immensely proud of having been able to provide me with an experience I clearly relished. When he went to the toilet I slipped a fifty dollar bill into the usual place in his backpack. I normally gave him only ten or twenty dollars, but was feeling happy and some-what elated at the end of a very long day, and I wanted to recognise the effort and sacrifice he had made.

Later that afternoon, an hour or so after he had dropped me at my hotel, there was an unexpected knock at my door and, opening it, I saw Kimly standing there, his face stern, even angry. 'You put fifty dollars into my bag today,' he said, pulling the money from his pocket and thrusting it at me. 'You made a mistake.'

'No, I didn't,' I said. 'I wanted to give you a gift. You've been so good and helpful to me.'

'I cannot accept this,' he responded, his voice shaking with emotion. 'We are friends. You are not paying me, I am not for sale. I don't want your money. Stop giving me money.' He was so emotional and so angry that I was actually frightened. I was also mortified. Kimly was far from avaricious, and I knew he was possessed of an enormous frailty that he masked with a suffocating pride.

I took the money from him and begged his forgiveness.

THE FRUIT GIRLS

Cambodia is, perhaps surprisingly, not really a great place for foodies. The Cambodians, though they take more pleasure in fruit than any other nation I have ever visited, have none of the more general interest in food evinced by the Vietnamese, Chinese or Thai. I didn't know anyone who was really interested in food or what they ate. People were far more interested in the 'class' of restaurant they were eating in, its cleanliness, clientele and appearance—for obvious reasons of status. Panit, for example, loved going to the Black Canyon Thai restaurant at the Paragon Centre, a ritzy but almost entirely deserted shopping mall in Phnom Penh. The food at the restaurant was tasty enough, but I was perplexed by his passion for the place. 'It makes me feel like I am eating somewhere high class,' he explained, as we took the seat by the window he always insisted on.

The window seat was good because it afforded us a view of the promotions and entertainments the centre hosted in the deserted carpark in an effort to drum up custom. One week was an unexpectedly popular 'Thai Fruit Expo' in which all the same fruits that grow in Cambodia were imported from Thailand and sold at great extra cost in cellophane-wrapped packets. People couldn't get enough. Even better, and wildly adored by the audience of mostly young people, were the nightly 'Thai Fruit Girls' spectaculars. These consisted of six Thai drag queens dressed as different tropical fruits, doing some very low-energy lip-synching to Thai pop songs.

It would have been hot inside those polystyrene fruit costumes and Miss Mangosteen, the oldest and sourest of the gang of gender-illusionists, felt her fate particularly keenly. She shouted and barked at her troupe, regularly sending Miss Rambutan back to change her laddered stockings (her costume wreaked havoc on tights), and refusing to go on until all of the slops had been mopped off the stage from the cooking demonstration that had preceded them.

Late one evening I was on my nightly constitutional to the Phnom Penh Mart at the corner of my street. The Love Orange nightclub downstairs from my room was having an open-mic hip hop night, and the vibrations literally shook through my body, making sleep elusive. I had imagined the Love Orange club was something quite glamorous and dangerous, though I never once set foot in the establishment. The security staff and DJs were all great pals of mine, seeing each other nightly as we did. Indeed, their knowledge of my night-time movements was quite encyclopaedic, and all friends had to do was drive past on their motorcycles and call out to the Love Orange bouncers to ask if I was home or not. This represented huge savings on their phone bills, not to mention enormous convenience.

The name of the club had captured my imagination. I found it quite zen-like in its opacity. Could it be making some poetic, veiled reference that lost all semblance of meaning in English? Was orange love some romantic description of sexual obsession in Khmer? Finally I remembered to ask one of my friends as we walked past the sign in daylight. 'What's "Love Orange" mean?' I asked, preparing myself to be educated.

My friend studied the sign carefully and said, 'It means "Love Orange".'

'Yes, but what on earth does "Love Orange" mean?' I asked

My friend looked at me in confusion. 'It means what it says, "to love oranges", you know, the fruit.'

This was no explanation at all. If anything, it deepened the mystery. 'But why on earth would someone call a nightclub "Love Orange"?' I asked.

'Probably the owner really loves oranges,' said my friend as we walked on.

So that night I was headed to the Phnom Penh Mart, the convenience store-cum-bar-cum-late-night refuge for insomniacs, drunkards and the criminally insane. As in convenience stores all over the world, the Phnom Penh Mart was lit at theatrical levels, and could be seen from some distance. Planes could probably have navigated from the light pouring out of Phnom Penh Mart's windows. It was really the most ghastly place to spend any time. That light guaranteed that anyone would look hideous.

As I strolled in I noticed, seated bored on the benches that ran along the windows, a gang of six androgynes. They were dressed in flip-flops, black shorts, roomy T-shirts and wide headbands that pushed the hair away from their scrubbed faces and almost invisible eyebrows. It was the after-hours uniform of performing drag queens the world over, a look I would recognise anywhere. For

people who make a living dressing extravagantly, cultivated slovenliness during leisure time becomes a point of
professional pride, a few hours of comfortable clothing
moments to be truly treasured.

I hadn't seen all that many drag queens in Phnom
Penh, though I knew a sub-culture existed, as it did
everywhere. I was watching them with curiosity when
the tallest one turned around and I recognised her in
an instant: the perpetual snarl, the slightly pitted face,
the hard jaw. It was none other than Miss Mangosteen,
reigning queen of the Thai Fruit Girls. Going over to
them, I introduced myself. 'Terrific show tonight,
ladies,' I said, holding out my hand. They were sweet
and chatty, drinking beers and eating from foaming
styrofoam bowls of two-minute noodles on the bench
in front of them. It was not hard to see that this was
a pretty shitty assignment. A bargain-basement novelty
act in a third-world hell-hole not all that far from home.

The adorable and flirtatious Miss Durian was
bubbling over with enthusiasm, however. 'My first international job,' she said, smiling with pride. 'After this one
maybe Dubai or Singapore, maybe a cruise ship—maybe
even your country. You think you could get me a job as
a *kathoey*?'

Not wanting to appear churlish, I lied. 'Oh sure,'
I said breezily. 'I'm sure something would come up.'

Miss Mangosteen was bored, and she fixed me with
a look and said, 'Come outside with me. I want to have

a cigarette.' Cowed into obedience in the face of such authority, I followed her and the security guard pulled up two plastic chairs for us, treating the ageing queen with great chivalry. It was hot and still in the Phnom Penh night and I could hear the muffled bass of the Love Orange club even at this distance. Our chairs faced an almost completely deserted intersection. Apart from the nightclub areas catering to tourists, Phnom Penh is a town that pretty much closes up at 9.30 p.m. 'This is the worst job,' she said, her eyes squinting and hardening as she dragged on her cigarette. She was more mature than the rest, perhaps in her late forties.

'I used to work in Pattaya—one of the big cabarets. But now too old, too ugly,' she said, smiling at her own cruel observation. She turned to look at me and, for a moment, there was friendliness, even softness, in her eyes. We were strangers together, middle-aged misfits in an odd little city not our own. 'Where are you staying?' she asked.

'At the Sakura Hotel, just up the road,' I answered.

She laughed. 'We are there too! What a dump! I was furious when I saw it. They make us stay in terrible places.'

Miss Durian pushed her face up against the glass behind us, and all the other queens laughed. I looked in on her and smiled and waved. 'You like her?' asked Miss Mangosteen, bemused, curious. 'She is young and silly—but very beautiful, I know. She gets all the boys.'

'Well, I'm not really looking,' I said.

'Really?' she said, fixing me with another stare. After a moment's hesitation she said, 'Maybe I can come and visit you tonight? You look like a nice man. Fat. I like fat.' Embarrassed, I laughed, as I always reflexively do. Her face fell back into its guarded hardness, and I realised I had been oafish. I had hurt her feelings when I hadn't meant to.

'It's not that I don't want to . . .' I stammered, shifting myself into even trickier territory. 'It's just . . . like I said, I am not really looking.'

'Well,' she said, brusque now, professional. She stood up to head back inside. 'If you change your mind we are in 416. All of us. One fucking room, the cheap bastards.'

PRAYER BREAKFAST IN SVAY SISOPHON

At the bus station on the day I was travelling to Banteay Meanchey I was served quickly and smilingly. My frequent trips with the same company meant that all the staff knew me now, and treated me with affection. Apart from being hideously dangerous, bus travel in Cambodia is cheap and not too daunting. The buses are all big, and the Cambodians are small and quiet, and rarely smoke, so make good travelling companions. The major drawback is the thing that is meant to be most diverting—the noisy 1980s Hong Kong movies dubbed into Khmer that are played at maximum volume on TVs attached to the roof above the driver. The noise is truly awful, but most of the passengers seemed to enjoy the entertainment, and even I was drawn in during particularly ridiculous films.

But on this occasion I found myself seated next to the biggest and fattest man I had ever encountered in Cambodia. He had none of the regular fat traveller's talent for making himself smaller, and so I faced eight hours of travelling most uncomfortably, the great bulk of me spilling out over the side of the seat and into the aisle. I know that the seating had been purely accidental, but there was no escaping the reality of two enormous people jostling for space on an eight-hour bus trip. It was made worse by the fact that, thirty minutes into the trip, my seat fell apart, the back rest falling completely away and nearly crushing the small boy and his tiny grandmother who were sitting behind me. They said absolutely nothing, merely stared at me fearfully with enormous eyes. I called the bus attendant, and he apologetically removed the errant back rest and stowed it in the front of the bus, near the driver. For the next seven and a half hours I would need to sit upright on my backless seat. By the time we arrived in Svay Sisaphon, the exquisitely named capital of Banteay Meanchey, I was almost crippled with pain.

My plus-sized companion carried on his person an ample supply of preserved mango strips and dried squid and in traffic jams when local village women jumped on the bus offering barbecued chicken and packets of sweet steamed rice, he availed himself of these as well. When he wasn't snacking, he was filling me in on the glories of the religion of Christ and his special relationship with that divine personage. He was a particularly enthusiastic Christian, and was keen that I might accompany him to some church-related events during my time away. I discovered over the ensuing hours that he was quite fired up about his new religious choice, and had a great deal to say about it in his unfortunately fluent English. I considered prevailing upon his sense of Christian ethics and asking him to swap seats, but in the end my shyness got the better of me.

He took particular relish in the word 'fellowship' and in the hours that we travelled together he used it an inordinate number of times. I became fixated with this peculiar repetition, and kept waiting for him to use it, or trying to coax him into saying it. 'Terrific fellowship in Banteay Meanchey,' he assured me, handing over a bag of boiled sweets for me to share.

'Really?' I said. 'How many Christians, exactly?'

'Many!' he assured me. 'Fourteen, fifteen . . . most work for the pastor.'

'And where does the pastor come from?' I asked.

'America,' he said, with great confidence. 'A very holy man. He has brought many souls to Jesus. I tell you what, when we get to Banteay Meanchey why don't you come with me and we'll go straight to his house. He would love to meet a writer.' I was seriously tempted by the offer, but I knew I was hardly the kind of person to inspire confidence in the good pastor.

'No,' I said politely. 'I cannot come. Besides, I don't think I'd be the kind of writer he'd like.'

'Why not?' asked my new friend.

'Well, I write about other religions, you see. Buddhism, for example.'

'Ah, Buddhism,' replied the plump man, his face theatrically sad. 'Yes, very bad religion. It is destroying my Cambodian people. Forget Buddhism, my friend— don't you fear for what will happen when you die? Don't write about such things, I beg you.'

When we finally arrived at Banteay Meanchey I was sore all over. I was also variously marked and smelly from the great variety of foods my seat mate had consumed. He, however, was in great good cheer, having arrived back at his spiritual heartland. He stayed by me as we retrieved our luggage and he beamed at my friend Phearun when he turned up to collect me. The two of them had a brief, animated and friendly chat in Khmer. Jumping onto the back of the bike, my bag balanced between my friend's legs at the front, I asked him what the chubby guy had been saying.

'Nice guy,' said my friend, supremely cool and free of judgement. 'Very friendly, but a bit strange. He told me Jesus loved me.' Phearun was a smiling and sweet young teacher I had met while he was spending the school holidays in Phnom Penh. He was laughing and apologetic about his town as we sped through the streets on the back of his motorcycle. 'This is a very boring place!' he said excitedly. 'Nothing at all to do here—you'll want to leave in a few hours, I can guarantee.'

But instead I was enchanted. Svay Sisophon was an exquisite and comfortable outpost about as far from Phnom Penh as it was possible to get without actually leaving the country. I'd found a sweet hotel with wifi, though Phearun was almost certain that no such thing existed there, and nearby delicious restaurants staffed by smiling, friendly people who had no English but were curious, happy and eager to please. I was almost instantly in love with the place, though I discovered on my second morning that I had selected the same hotel as my tubby Christian friend from the bus, and he bellowed at me from across the lobby: 'Join us for a prayer breakfast, brother?'

Phearun was somewhat disappointed in his job. Teachers in the Cambodian state system are paid a miserable pittance, and the country children and their parents showed very little interest in education. When the term started, the students often wouldn't show till the second or even third week of the semester, and after that their absences were frequent as their presence on the farm was deemed more important. 'They finish school and they know nothing at all,' complained Phearun. 'They can barely read, or add up, they have no knowledge of geography or history, most have never owned a book. Sometimes I feel ashamed of myself when I see my own students and how miserable their lives are.' His own status as teacher, however, was an elevated one in a rural community, and the same parents that kept their children away from school would send him elaborate and expensive gifts and hold banquets in his honour. 'They respect what I am, but they have no idea how to improve the lives of their own children,' he said.

It was the very hottest part of the hot season, but Svay Sisophon's relative quietness and its proximity to nature made it seem cooler than Phnom Penh, though everyone everywhere assured me this was not the case. I could walk around in the town, though not in the hottest hours, and I enjoyed this pretty little place, enjoyed my specialness and the absence of other tourists. I only encountered two other foreigners during my time there. One was a plump woman in an expensive hire car who, seeing a rubbish collection truck making its rounds, had the car stop in the middle of the street while she leaped out to take photographs of the rubbish collectors. This mystified Phearun. 'Crazy foreigners,' he said. 'Why on earth would you travel to another country to take photos of people picking up rubbish?' Why indeed, though I suspected that those shots might make up a colourful example of the 'poverty and filth' portfolio that many Western visitors to Cambodia like to build up.

I encountered the second foreigner when I was returning alone to my hotel after visiting a nearby pagoda. Now, I am by nature a reasonably shy person, and was always taught that it wasn't polite to speak to strangers without good reason. As I walked along the road a foreign man approached on a motorcycle, driving slowly with no helmet in the opposite direction. I am by no means snobbish, and would most certainly have returned the man's greeting had he directed one to me, but he was possessed instead of an unfriendly scowl and I assumed he was not interested in another lonely foreigner roaming the streets of an unlikely Cambodian town. So I affected a non-committal half-smile and middle-distance stare, the sort assumed by shopkeepers when walking across their floor. The man slowed his motorcycle after passing me, turned and drove up next to me.

'You're not one of them, you know!' he shouted, and I turned to look at him, startled. His face was a picture of inexplicable fury.

'Don't try to pretend,' he said as he sped away into the evening.

HOT, HOT!

We were experiencing a thirty-year record heat wave in the area. The daily average high in Bangkok that month was 40.1, and it wasn't much lower in Phnom Penh. I was finding it increasingly uncomfortable, even sickening, to get around. By the time I made it to the newspaper stands outside Wat Langka at 7 a.m. my clothes would be soaked in sweat, clinging unflatteringly to my ample curves. 'Hot, hot!' would call the heavily pregnant woman who sold me my papers, looking completely refreshed and beautiful, not a bead of perspiration on her brow. Once I discovered on her stall a Khmer translation of a self-help book I knew well, *The 21 Irrefutable Laws of Leadership* by John C Maxwell. Thinking it would be just the thing for a monk, I bought the book, which was incredibly cheap. After that day the stallholder made sure she always had copies in stock, and would casually throw one into my order, no matter what I was buying. I spread these involuntary purchases far and wide, and monks and visitors to the temple could often be seen carrying copies.

I find Cambodian Buddhist temples to be maddeningly under-capitalised. In Vietnam many temples in the cities contain bookshops, souvenir stalls and even restaurants. All manner of Buddhist-related tat can be purchased at any of Bangkok's major temples. But the visitors to Cambodia's most important places of worship leave empty handed and it is an enormous opportunity for some forward-thinking abbott. There were also no books in English about Cambodian Buddhism written by Cambodians. There are two exceptional ones in English by foreign academics, but again, there is a gap for a monk with good English to start writing from what must be an utterly unique Cambodian Buddhist perspective.

During the heat wave, I would stumble into the monastery and sit at a bench to read the *Cambodia Daily*, though by the third page it too would be damp from my sweating hands. I simply couldn't bear the heat. Because it was around exam time, groups of students would collect in one of the side buildings at the monastery while a favoured monk would chant blessings for them. I envied them the confidence of some supernatural edge to their day's efforts. Growing up a Methodist boy in small-town Australia, I had never enjoyed any such avenue for added assurance. Not for the first time I was admiring of the Cambodian religious system, which provided all manner of spiritual comforts in the face of decidedly materialistic endeavours.

I was constantly enchanted by the sight of monks coming back from their errands, their classes or their begging rounds. One of Cambodia's iconic images is the barefoot monks walking the streets in the morning begging for food and cash, their bright orange robes blazing in the sun, their picturesque umbrella in the exact same shade, a perfect foil to the glare and an impossibly elegant accessory. On these hot days, seeing them shaded from the sun under capacious umbrellas made me ache with jealousy—this practical solution was forbidden to me, as a Western man. I envied, too, the careful Korean and Chinese woman tourists who shielded themselves with a dazzling variety of umbrellas. Just as I was almost tempted to indulge myself in the purchase of a very practical and understated black umbrella, I happened to be with a group of friends when we encountered two pasty Western men walking down the street shaded by cheap red umbrellas. Everyone shrieked with a tantalised derision. 'Look at those fools!' they giggled. 'Walking around like grandmothers with their umbrellas. What kind of men are they? Do they not care how foolish they look? I'd say they needed a bit of sun to toughen them up.' I kept a shamefaced silence, glad that I'd held off a little before making my purchase.

Inside Wat Langka I had a dear but exasperating friend, a handsome monk in his thirties called Kosal. I was never very sure about why I was Kosal's friend. He spoke good English and was smiling and affable and he gave me insider's access to the workings of an enormous city temple, but I was strangely disturbed by my own motives for being so close to him. For, no matter how holy the occasion and how determined I was to keep my mind on elevated spiritual matters, the sheer brute force of Kosal's masculine beauty disturbed me, and it was something I dwelt on. The thin cotton robes and shaved head of the monk, intended to render the wearer anonymous and plain beyond vanity, were exactly the things that suited Kosal best, throwing into stark relief his big, exquisitely shaped skull, strong jaw and shining white teeth. The robe that left one shoulder and arm exposed left constantly visible one of the most perfect biceps I had ever seen, bulging from a lifetime's hard work.

Cambodian friends were impressed by my devotion to this monk, the time I spent with him and the support I offered, but more sophisticated friends would be suspicious the moment they laid eyes on him. 'Ooee!' screamed one camp friend when Kosal left the room after I had just introduced them. 'Now I know why you have suddenly become such a good Buddhist. I'm tempted to take the robes myself. Think he'll need another disciple once you've gone?'

But my dedication to Kosal remained necessarily chaste, and I was rewarded with greater access into the work and life of the monks. I conducted spontaneous English conversation clubs in Kosal's room, which would fill with monks keen to practise. I would have them translate for me the more luridly illustrated stories from the sensationalist newspapers, and all of us would be swept up in the outrageous tales of double-love suicides, the affairs of boxers and actresses and the petty swindling of small-town government officials. At the end of each story the monks would nod sagely and say things like, 'People behave very badly in Cambodia. They are not conscious of their karma.'

Wat Langka housed a small monastic academy that taught classes from primary through to high school level. This school taught the young monks the essentials of their religion, and Kosal was the principal of the high school. 'At primary school they study the *Dhammapada*,' he explained, naming the short but complete Buddhist text that is said to contain the essence of the Buddha's teachings. 'In middle school they study the *Visuddhimagga*, and then at high school I teach them the individual *suttas*, depending on what I think is appropriate.'

Kosal would show me into the locked rooms and halls of the monastery, many of them exquisitely decorated with gilded carvings and colourful murals, but all unused and reserved for special occasions, which never seemed to manifest. Instead, everything happened in the carpeted lower hall, a mercifully cool spot that was always open and normally filled with students, monks and the visiting faithful. Arriving at the lower hall one sweltering morning I was confronted with Kosal and a team of younger monks all doing some major cleaning. 'We have a big party today,' he said. 'We must get ready now, make the pagoda beautiful.'

As the day progressed, more and more people came to decorate the hall. A small gilded and elevated throne was placed in front of the main shrine, and quite enormous potted palms, bananas and other trees were installed all around. These were then hung with decorative bunches of fruit. Occasionally the trees bore incongruous fruit, sprouting a long garland of connected limes, or thick clusters of longans.

AV equipment turned up, and a menacing row of rock-concert speakers was attached to a microphone erected in front of the tiny throne. A trestle table was set up outside and a row of senior monks installed behind it in front of ledgers to record the donations of visitors. Then a traditional orchestra assembled itself in the back porch of the worship hall, and people began to arrive.

'Today we recite the life stories of the Buddha,' explained Kosal as he rolled up tiny fragments of scripture and put them in a large decorative silver bowl at the monks' table. These were to be the rewards for the generous—a piece of Buddhist wisdom that would serve as an oracle for the person who selected it. One by one the monks sat on the tiny wooden throne and, hands held before them in prayer position, they would recite one of the past-life stories of the Buddha from a tradition-ally bound text on their laps. These *Jataka* (*Cheadok* in Khmer) tales are colourful stories that are well known in the Buddhist world, and detail lives in which the Buddha was a deer or a lion, a king or a monkey. All served a moral lesson, indicating the value of generosity and sacrifice in the eternal effort to move up the karmic ladder.

A dozen or so monks sat around the throne on a rotating roster. The visual effect, though, was marred by the restlessness of the young monks who variously drank Cokes, waved to friends and family in the audience or took calls on their mobiles. The real stars were the child monks, the little ones of nine or ten who ascended the rickety throne and droned their way through the set text in a boyish soprano in stark contrast to the affected bass of the older monks. Each stumble and mispronunciation caused a gasp of adoration in the audience. As these little fellows ended their gig there was always one or two people in the audience who would clap, only to be shushed by nearby nuns.

I'd been keen to take part in this religious celebration, but as day turned into night and seemed only to get hotter, I was beginning to flag, and my position on the cement floor was becoming increasingly tortured and ungraceful. Kosal came by and handed me a banana and a hot can of Red Bull. 'When does it finish?' I asked as he squatted down next to me and beamed at me with his movie star smile.

'Who knows?' he answered. 'Six hours, ten, twelve— it depends on when we finish the stories.'

'But will all these people stay here?' I asked, gesturing at the audience made up largely of elderly women with cropped silver hair and lacy white blouses. They had all been sitting quietly and attentively for some hours now. Surely none of them could handle another twelve?

'Many of them will,' said Kosal. 'The best ones. But mostly people come and go, an hour here, an hour there. The monks are the same. This is meant to be fun!'

Popping the energy drink and mostly green banana into my bag, I made an effort to stand up, but the hours cross-legged on the floor had paralysed me, and I collapsed back down again, narrowly missing a tiny nun sitting nearby. The worshippers around us laughed, and one old lady reached over and pinched my arm in sympathy. Identifying through body language that it was my enormous gut that had caused this temporary paralysis, the women nearby showed me what positions I could assume that would be inoffensive and also allow blood flow to return to my feet.

Kosal manifested again suddenly, having been quickly informed by a chain of whispers that I wasn't doing so well. 'Are you OK?' he asked. 'They said you fell.'

'I didn't so much fall as couldn't get up,' I said. Smiling he reached down to me and pulled me to my feet in a completely un-monklike gesture. But no-one seemed scandalised by this act of kindness, and I was left leaning against one of the temple columns, gasping at the almost-pain of pins and needles rushing through my lower extremities.

'Ha ha, you are too fat, brother,' said Kosal, completely unaware of the fuss and noise we were causing in our little corner of the audience. 'Come, up to the front and bow to the Buddha and say goodbye to the monks so people can see you.' I was suddenly part of the festivities, and was lead through the crowded hall, treading on people's hands and feet as I made my way up to the main platform. I squatted and performed the ritual bows with a complete absence of grace, though as an act it caused a ripple of approval and admiration from the audience, the exact effect Kosal had hoped for. A few of the monks I knew clambered over to the edge of the dais to say goodbye though the recitation was still going on in full volume just a metre above their heads.

Knowing I was leaving they began to pull gifts for me out of the bags of offerings that had been made to them. A sweltering can of 7Up, a bottle of green oil and a packet of Oreos were all thrust into my hand. Kosal reached up and pulled an entire pineapple from a bunch that seemed to be growing from a potted fig tree. 'Go safely, brother,' he said, handing me the inconvenient fruit. 'And stay cool.'

I always feel most at ease with monks, and there was some kind of past-life connection which made me see my monk friend Kosal as more than just an exotically robed figure of distraction. I felt he was a brother, in a most intense and real way. The restrictions of his religious lifestyle affected the way we could interact, the times and circumstances in which we could see each other, and yet there was a passion and intensity to our friendship which went beyond its arbitrary, and short-term, nature. As always in Cambodia, I was inspired and impressed by his tremendous sweetness, the energy he cultivated in thinking about his future, which was most definitely not to be played out in a monastery.

Though Kosal was in his early thirties and had been living as a monk since a teenager, the future he envisioned was thoroughly worldly. It involved a wife, children and a high-paying job, and these things he discussed with me quite frankly, as did all the other monks. It came as an initial shock that they weren't spending their waking hours contemplating the nature of existence. Instead they studied for their English exams or went to IT courses. They kept in touch with their girlfriends back in their home villages via their mobile phones.

'My family is big,' explained Kosal. 'We live in a border town near Vietnam, and my father is old. I could stay at the farm and be a poor man forever, or I could come to Phnom Penh and be a monk and improve my life. For me it was no choice. For a while I must sacrifice the things that men love—beer, women, a free life. But soon I can have all that and be in a much better position than if I'd just run after it as a young man.' Kosal had used his time as a monk wisely. He had become a trusted member of the monastic community, had learned

English and earned an undergraduate degree. He had saved money and he was at the point of being ready to embark on his worldly life.

One day I strolled into the grounds of Wat Langka and there, sitting on the cement benches outside the monks' quarters where I spent so many of my mornings, was a big, dark-skinned man with a shaved head. He was dressed in an awful pair of made-in-China polyester slacks that were too tight and short, and an equally awful and cheap short-sleeved shirt. His white sports socks were clearly visible in the gap left by his too-short trousers, and they were pushed into a ghastly pair of faux-leather loafers. Such men were not unusual at temples. They were normally country hicks visiting their monk brothers. But this one stood up, fixed me with a dazzling white smile and said, 'Brother, don't you recognise me?'

It was Kosal, the beautiful, regal Kosal, majestic among his brother monks and set apart by his ethereal beauty in robes. Now he was ugly, the exquisitely strong body clumsy in its cheap clothes. He looked more of a bumpkin than any recently arrived country boy. After seventeen years in robes he had no idea how to wear real clothes, and he fidgeted and pulled at his uncomfortable new garments.

Each pocket bulged with a cheap mobile phone, and they kept falling out as we sat there chatting. The pockets were too tight to hold anything properly, and the white lining gaped visibly as he sat. He clutched to his chest a monk-orange plastic envelope. 'You look so surprised. I told you it was almost the end for me. I wanted to leave straight after the Khmer New Year. I am going on job interviews!' he cried, holding aloft that orange envelope which had once carried his papers to the Buddhist Institute.

Despite all his goofiness and his unrealistic expectation, I couldn't help but admire Kosal. He was moving towards his dream. He had great hope in a set of circumstances where I would probably hold none. I wished that I had possessed his optimism and certitude when I'd been his age. What lay in store for this strange-looking man? A job, certainly, but probably not the elevated one he wanted and expected. A girlfriend, perhaps. 'But not in the near future,' he explained. 'At least not until my hair has grown back. Besides, Cambodian girls won't look at someone who is poor, so I may have quite a wait ahead of me when it comes to finding a wife. But don't worry about that—I have survived this long without one.'

Kosal, who up until that morning had been my spiritual advisor, was still my superior in every way. That huge, toothy smile was set towards the future, and he refused to allow worry to weigh him down. Kosal was moving on.

GOING BACK
TO SIEM REAP

Given that the hot season was at its most terrible and I could barely cope any longer with the warm winds of Phnom Penh, I decided to take up a friend's invitation to return to Siem Reap and spend some of my final days in Cambodia in the town that is the only one so many tourists to Cambodia ever see.

Soon after settling into an undeservedly plush hotel, I went for a massage at a luxuriously appointed day spa by the river, the kind of place that seems reassuringly legitimate. There are many things that the male traveller has to consider when seeking genuine massage in Asia—it can be a surprisingly tricky quest. I have found from experience that places that seem to have staff of both genders hanging about are normally more trustworthy, and when I went into this place I was further reassured by the presence of the actual masseuses. They were stocky middle-aged women, unmade-up, the type who looked as though they would brook no hanky-panky. I handed over my money for an hour-long massage with an untroubled conscience.

My conscience was to stay that way, but it was an altogether odd encounter. My matronly therapist, who spoke quite good English, peppered me with any number of disconcerting questions, posed loudly in an area where customers were screened from each other only by tasteful muslin curtains. 'Have you got a mistress?' was her opening question. Not a wife, mind, or even girl-friend. She wanted to get straight to the scandal. When I assured her I hadn't she seemed disbelieving. I blushed as my face was pushed down into a pillow.

She was plump, indeed she was slipping out of plump and approaching fat, but she complained bitterly about my own physique, something I'd never experienced at the hands of a masseuse before. 'Too fat!' she shrieked as she grabbed whatever excess flesh was nearest to hand as she made her point. She decided that the only way she could manage my bulk was by walking on me, which, due to her own impressive weight, was an absolute agony. I finally convinced her to dismount, which she did with a tremendous sigh of annoyance, and then she began to torture me with her thumbs, wrist and elbows. The whole treatment was the opposite of relaxing, and I began to pray that it would be over soon.

Flipping me over onto my back with her considerable upper-body strength, she shrieked so loudly that nearby masseuses began to giggle and, seizing one of my nipples she began to laugh herself. 'Such a big fat man, but such tiny teats,' she cried, before calling it out in Khmer to everyone nearby. The teal muslin curtains began to twitch and flap as nearby workers decided to peer in for a look at my apparently unnaturally small nipples. Now, I am not a man who is particularly confident about his body, and there are any number of its parts that I could single out at any given moment for some pretty harsh criticism. But up until this point I was reasonably happy with the size of my nipples. I had always assumed they were more or less inoffensive.

But now I had a whole new thing to worry about, and, coming home smelling of naturally derived ginger and cardamom, I spent some time at my mirror investigating these tiny pink lumps from every angle. When I got bored with that I discovered the deep blue bruises that had formed along my arms and between my shoulders. My hearty masseuse had evidently used a too firm hand in my treatment. Or the bruises could have been derived from the ten minutes or so she spent trampling over me—there was a black spot right in the middle of my back that I could swear looked like a pudgy footprint.

The editor of *New Dawn* magazine had told me that there was a temple in Siem Reap devoted to a *Naga* spirit, and that it sat directly behind the Pyramid nightclub. I knew it was a place I had to visit. The ancient Khmer believed in dragons, *Naga* and water spirits. The *Naga* exist throughout South-East Asia, half-dragon, half-snake and often hydra-headed. They are ancient and oddly recognisable representatives of a truly global symbol that manifests both as the wicked and violent dragons of Western mythology and as the lucky and auspicious symbols of China and Vietnam. The *Naga* king, representative of an antique folk religion, was deftly adopted by Buddhists when they made him a part of the story of the Buddha. While Shakyamuni Buddha sat beneath the Bodhi tree, intent on enlightenment, it began to pour with rain, and the *Naga* king, taking pity on this brave, determined figure, twisted his body around the Buddha and opened up his enormous, multi-headed hood to create a canopy for the Buddha's protection.

In Cambodia the image of the *Naga* is everywhere, and one is conscious that the respect and worship for this mythological creature goes back much further and deeper than the age of Buddhism. The king of Cambodia was once said to have been formally married to a *Naga* princess, and Cambodian brides of wealthy families once wore capes recreating the *Naga*'s scales when they first went to bed with their new husbands. His image is all over the Angkor ruins, his heads flaring up at the ends of balustrades, both greeting and warning visitors.

The site is actually just a regular Cambodian Buddhist temple, a *wat*, and a particularly poor and decrepit one at that. The *vihara*, the main religious building in the complex which houses the central Buddha image, was a wooden shack put together crudely with unfinished planks that had warped and split over the years, leaving gaps between them large enough to look through. But it sits on ancient ground, and behind the main monastery complex, on a small hill, is a little cool shrine, built around an Angkorean-period carving of a *Naga*'s head. The shrine is new and kind of gaudy, tiled in an inappropriate manner, but is situated perfectly to catch any breeze—an important consideration when you are living in a town as hot as Siem Reap. This carved head is not, however, any regular antique. The old blind nun who attends the shrine and tells fortunes to visiting devotees told me that at night this particular statue comes to life and the *Naga* can be seen sliding over the cool tiles and enjoying the pool of fresh, clear water that has been provided for him in front of the altar.

At night no-one will come near the shrine, not even the nun who has attended it for a decade or more, for this *Naga* was once a fearsome spirit who ruled the land all around. Three hundred years ago a strong young Buddhist monk had come to establish a temple for the farmers living here. He was warned, however, to stay away.

'This whole area belonged to the *Naga*,' said the nun. 'And he would regularly take people and eat them. The villagers lived in fear, terrified to let their children wander freely. But the young abbott would not be swayed. He climbed this hill and built a cage. That night he began to chant and, drawn by the strange sound and the provocative presence of a foolish human, the *Naga* approached.

As he heard the Buddhist prayers he became hypnotised and the monk led him easily into the cage. Once the *Naga* was inside, the monk slammed the doors shut and he has been here ever since.'

She gestured towards the iron bars that trapped the stone statue of the *Naga*'s head. I suddenly felt sorry for the poor creature, locked for centuries in its cramped cage while the villagers lived freely around it. 'But that's why we pray to it now,' explained the nun. 'People come from all over Cambodia to make offerings and pray to him. Phnom Penh, Battambang—even overseas. California! The *Naga* is still a powerful being and can offer help to those who pay their respects to him.' She began to list the miracles, a recognisable litany of good fortune: children healed, surgery survived, exams passed, overseas jobs found. So powerful was this *Naga*, trapped in the base of a shrine covered with statues of Lord Buddha, that small replicas of him were found on the shrines of all the important temples in Siem Reap.

I was so taken by this sacred site, so aware of its powerful 'vibe', that I told my friends in Phnom Penh about it. They all scoffed. None of them had heard of the shrine, so it obviously wasn't as famous as the old nun had suggested. My friend Kakkada laughed at me. 'So you're telling me the *Naga* comes to life at night? You don't think that kind of thing would get onto TV pretty quickly if it was true? Boy, I thought Cambodians were gullible . . .'

But when we visited the temple together, Kakkada was bowed and silent. His eyes glowed as the old nun recounted the same stories and he stayed kneeled in front of the altar for a long time, saying his prayers. When he was finished we both sat on the cool tiles with the nun and Kakkada asked her about her life, translating her answers for me. Soon her blind eyes wept as she laid out her tale of sorrow.

'Before Pol Pot days I had a family—a husband, three children. We all lived in a big house in Siem Reap with my brother. When we had to leave I tried so hard to stay together with my family, but eventually it was impossible. One by one we were separated until all had gone. And I never saw any of them again, not my husband, not my children. All dead, I have to assume.' She picked up the small bundle of palm-leaf pages inscribed with sayings of the Buddha. These were her stock in trade, the instruments she used for telling people's fortunes.

'I went back to Siem Reap, once we could go back. I lived in the garden of what had once been our house— the people who had taken the house wouldn't let me inside. I waited and waited for my family to return, but none ever came. Then one day my brother turned up. The new people chased him down the street but I followed, though later I wished I hadn't. He was mad, you see—filthy and raving, completely crazy. He had no idea who I was. I tried to tell him but he stared at me

and walked away. Who knows, perhaps he's still alive.
I always pray for him.'

Wiping away her tears, she beamed out at us, tooth-
less, her deeply etched face and the fine white stubble
over her scalp all completely beautiful. 'Ask the foreign
man if he wants his fortune told,' she instructed Kakkada.

'But she's blind,' I said, worried. 'How on earth can
she tell what card she has?'

After we had selected our first hard little palm-leaf
card, Kakkada read out the first couple of words and the
old nun finished the rest of the phrase. 'I knew I was
going blind—it was obvious. And so I came out here
and prayed to the *Naga* to give me back my sight. I was
so poor—I had nothing, nowhere to stay. So that night
I slept in the vegetable garden at the monastery. The
Naga came to me in my dreams and said, "Become a
nun, you wicked old woman. Your karma is heavy, and
this is the only way you can right things for your next life.
And stop wasting time! Memorise the scriptures—they
will save you." For a long time I didn't understand what
he meant by that. I built a hut in the vegetable garden
and lived there, tending to the plants. Then, one night,
a woman came to my hut. I didn't know her; perhaps
she had once been one of the *Naga*'s wives. She was old,
but still beautiful. She gave me my first set of palm-leaf
scriptures.

'"Memorise these, old woman," she said. "You are
going blind and how are you to live once that happens?

If you can remember these scriptures you can be of assistance to people and they will help you stay alive." And so I did. Day after day I read them and tried to commit them to memory, but, oh! It was hard. The hardest thing I have ever done in my life. I can work in the hot sun all day, but I was never any kind of scholar. But every day I came up here and swept and cleaned the *Naga*'s shrine and I told him all about my worries, and so every night he would come to me in my dreams and teach me the scriptures.

'People started to come, more and more of them. Some Khmer living in America had some good luck and paid to have the shrine renovated and made beautiful, as you see it now. And then the day came when I simply couldn't read the palm-leaf pages any more. But I found that all I needed to do was ask the person what the first words were, and all the rest come flooding out. He had saved me,' she said, pointing towards the caged carving.

Before we left, Kakkada opened his wallet and gave the nun all of the money he had in it. She pushed forward her small square of beautifully woven cloth and we left the offering there, delicately avoiding placing the cash directly into her hands, an act that would be unseemly for a religious woman.

In the tuk tuk on the way back into town Kakkada was quiet. 'So,' I asked, 'what do you think of the *Naga*?'

'True or not true, who knows?' he said. 'But I am Khmer. I must believe.'

FALLING IN WITH
THE RIGHT CROWD

As we made our way through the market we bumped
into Chan, a young man who composed beautiful songs
and occupied the outermost limits of the writing scene
in Phnom Penh. Chan was tiny in stature, a result of his
childhood malnourishment, and he sought to compensate for this by an extreme athleticism. He studied
martial arts, Cambodian boxing and weight lifting and
he rode his bicycle—the only vehicle he could afford—at
a breakneck speed wherever he went. He could cross the
city in twenty minutes. This excessive devotion to sports
had rendered him extravagantly muscular: his neck and
shoulder muscles bulged out of his clothing and his
enormous pecs and biceps sat somewhat awkwardly on
his naturally compact frame.

Charming, funny and, in his own strange way, attractive, Chan was a clever orphan boy who had discovered
a respectable community once he'd been forced to
leave his institution. What could have gone so horribly
wrong had, in Chan's case, somehow been made right,
and he had done that rarest of things—fallen in with
the right crowd. Other writers pitched in money for

Chan to attend classes at the cheap community college run by the monks at the Buddhist Institute, and he always took out the certificates of merit in composition, English, Buddhist studies and Khmer literature. 'Look,' said Tola, pointing to a small, immaculately groomed head bobbing low through the crowd. 'There's your friend, that poor, miserable boy.' The description, while confronting and condescending to an English speaker, was perfectly appropriate in a Cambodian context. Chan's goodness in the face of hardship meant that he inhabited a special position in the eyes of his peers, someone who had overcome their karma and so proved a Buddhist lesson.

Chan's major occupation at this stage was selling newspapers and magazines on a corner of Monivong Boulevard, supplemented by extra work in the fledgling Cambodian film industry, where a strong and agile man of his diminutive stature was surprisingly in demand. Because of his occupation, Chan was remarkably well informed about current events, or at least the current events that the Khmer-language newspapers chose to report. Chan knew of every recent death, rape and suicide, right down to the streets and suburbs involved. But despite his keenness and application, none of his sources of income seemed to ever combine to much at all, and it was still whispered that Chan lived on the streets, paying to bathe at the pagodas and storing his valuables with sympathetic friends. Nonetheless he managed to turn up unfailingly to religious and cultural events, always perfectly dressed, spotlessly clean and smiling.

'Sir, sir!' he cried, waving an arm in the air as we approached. He always called me sir, though it made me feel uncomfortable. A year or so before, soon after meeting him for the first time, he had come with friends to join me for lunch at KFC, his first experience of Western food. Naturally he had found it almost inedible, and I watched fascinated as he pushed the pieces of fried chicken onto the plates of his more worldly friends and instead ate the accompanying rice and two slices of tomato. Having been informed of his story, and of his great resilience and honesty, I took a special interest in him, and when everyone else prepared to go I had asked him to stay with me and go and have coffee. Walking along beside his bike, we chatted—he had remarkable English, which he constantly practised and cultivated. Alone in the coffee shop I slipped him two fifty dollar bills as unobtrusively as possible and this, after I'd been to the toilet and he'd had time to check how much I'd given, caused him to cry.

'No one in my life has ever given me this much money,' he said, his face crumpled. Later, after I left Cambodia, he had emailed me a detailed account of what he'd done with the money. I don't think I've ever spent a hundred dollars more wisely. But this act had cemented our relationship in some kind of official way, and from that moment I had become Chan's sponsor, a role taken very seriously in Cambodia. This meant that I was to be treated not as a friend or an older brother, even an uncle. My status became the same as that of a father, and he had to treat me with the according formality.

THE FORTUNE TELLER

I had for some time been preoccupied with fortune tellers in Phnom Penh. I wanted to try all of the ones that hung about in all of the major city temples, elderly men and women who held little handfuls of palm-leaf manuscripts etched with quotes from the Buddhist scriptures that acted as oracles. The meaning of each passage changed according to the seeker's situation. Taking the bundle, I would hold it to my head three times while I prayed to the Buddha. Each time I had to place a small bamboo marker in the place I was drawn to. Then the three passages were laid out on the floor and the fortune teller began to discuss the possibilities of meaning.

Normally Mak came along with me, patiently translating the passages and the reading from the fortune teller. But he never once consulted the oracle himself. 'My family believe that whatever you hear from these people must come true,' he explained. 'That's why I don't want to hear anything. What if he says something bad? Then I am doomed. I'd rather not know.'

Right near where I lived was a sign attached to the electricity pole pointing down an alleyway. Though I couldn't read Khmer I knew it was advertising the services of a fortune teller: the sign featured a large image of the fat Buddha of the future, surrounded by the twelve animals of the Chinese zodiac. One afternoon I convinced my friend Mak to come with me down the alley and find the fortune teller's premises. Once we found the house that had the same sign, we went in through the open door and made our way up the stairs, coming upon a verandah that was decorated like a small Chinese temple, with an enormous and elaborate shrine, in front of which was a table laid with a yellow cloth and scattered with the paraphernalia of fortune telling: a magnifying glass, an abacus, a deck of cards and any number of lucky objects. We sat on the heavy, elaborate Chinese chairs and nobody at all came. 'This is spooky,' said Mak.

Finally an elderly woman popped her head up over the stairs and asked if we wanted the fortune teller. 'He's not here,' she said. 'He's at his other shop. Wait and I'll get someone to take you.' She came back quickly with a tiny lesbian who drove us to a distant market on a tuk tuk.

We were dropped outside a shop that sold religious supplies for monks, objects of good luck and the ubiquitous statue of the waving woman that is said to bring in customers. We were ushered behind a curtain, and there sat the master. He was seated on a luxuriously appointed couch in front of a low Chinese table cluttered with the tools of his trade. A tremendously obese Chinese man, he sat sweating wildly and smoking a cigarette through a filter. These cigarettes kept going, and he lit one from the other, which explained the half-dozen full ashtrays dotted about him. He also burned a pungent incense.

Absolutely everything in this parlour was covered with a layer of grey dust. It was hard to know if the dust came from his cigarettes, the constantly burning incense, or the Johnson & Johnson's baby powder he would pick up intermittently and puff all over his front. He had an immensely fat neck, with great sweaty rolls that obviously troubled him. It was to these he applied the talcum powder, attempting to stave off heat rash. At either side of him were brass spittoons, and these too he made liberal use of, leaning one way or another to hack out something. I suspect he was an asthmatic, because when he began to speak to us, with a great deal of nervous energy, his voice was gravelly, high-pitched and wheezy.

Mak's eyes widened when he saw the room, and when the fortune teller began to speak. 'Look,' he said to me, pointing out the baby powder. 'He's just like you.' It's true that I am also a great lover of talc. I find it an enormous comfort and a thriftily sensuous pleasure. I have also come to realise, over the years, the unchallenged superiority of Johnson & Johnson's Baby Powder, especially a variety I have only ever seen in Thailand (and exported to Cambodia and Vietnam) that contains milk—it is delicious. But I loved Cambodia because Tabu talcum powder was also still available, an iconic 1970s bathroom item in its black tin container with the painting of a Flamenco dancer. I concealed in my room (it was hardly the most manly item) my own container, and I regularly bought more to give to friends' mothers. As a powder it couldn't beat Johnson & Johnson's classic, but it made up for it with the most beautiful scent, which people regularly commented on.

The fortune teller began the consultation almost as soon as we walked through the door, and Mak did his best to translate the high-speed patter of the clairvoyant. But his translation suffered because, possessed of a novelist's ear, Mak was fascinated by the mechanics and structure of the man's speech. 'He uses the language of a woman,' he told me, and I had already noticed him using the feminine affirmation 'Jaa'. This was also a habit of royalty in Cambodia, but neither of us had ever encountered a common man who dared to do it.

Grabbing my hands, the fortune teller put my palms up and cleaned them with a cloth and a small bottle of cheap after-shave. The same thing had to be done to the soles of my feet, which he also read. Using an enormous, theatrical magnifying glass, he consulted the lines and dimples on my face and calculated the distance between my nose and ears, my eyes and chin. Then he pulled my head forward and peered at my crown through his glass. Then, requesting my birth date, he pulled out a huge black wood abacus and began to make some calculations.

There was a theatrical pause while he sat with his figures, and Mak and I both leaned forward to catch the results of all this examination. Blinking up at us through his thick glasses, he lit another cigarette, shook a puff of powder over his neck fat and then lobbed a great green lump into the direction of one of the spittoons. 'Not all good, not all bad,' he declared somberly. 'Anyone can see the man has good luck—look at the size of him, and his fat face. You didn't need to come to me to know that. But there will be no real success for him until 2015. He's like a vine that grows circularly and gradually rather than a tree that shoots up straight. But he is resilient, like an island—this is a man who has no need for religion.'

As he spoke he pulled out a square of white cotton and began to assemble my own personal fetish. He placed inside the white cloth a red *yon*, the magical talismans common in Cambodia. Then, from a box next to the table, he took a small plastic dog and what looked like a spaceman, wrapped them in the yon and bound them together with red cotton. After this he wrapped the package loosely in the white cloth. When he handed it to me he told me to hold it in both hands while he sprayed it with the same cheap perfume that he'd used to cleanse my hands and feet. Then he did some kind of chant in Chinese dialect, and then the *Namo Tassa* Buddhist incantation three times.

'To this package,' he explained, 'I want you to add a cloth clipping from a shirt you wear often. Then take some hair from every part of your body.' At this he paused modestly and added, 'and I do mean every part of your body. Then include some toenail and fingernail clippings, an old shirt and an old pair of pants, and 5000 riel in 100 riel notes. This bundle you then need to throw into running water—the river in front of the king's palace is the best, but any running water will do.'

My mind rebelled at this. The front of the king's palace was a pretty heavily policed stretch of water, and I could only imagine their reaction to a foreigner throwing a strange and lumpy bundle into it in the middle of the night. 'I cannot come with you when you do this!' he suddenly shrieked. It was obviously an important point. 'Don't even ask me—this is something only you can do.' In truth I hadn't been planning on suggesting this rather repellant man accompany me anywhere in public, but he still needed to make this clear, so he repeated it several times.

'And that's it,' he said, falling back exhausted, as though he'd done some particularly heavy lifting. I thought it had been a minimal kind of effort, but he ran a cloth across his beaded brow and reached behind him to grab a beer, which he popped open. The stench of the parlour was incredible, and I desperately wanted to get out. But I knew we hadn't yet come to the most delicate part of the exercise: paying. Mak made a casual and polite enquiry about the price, and the fortune teller snorted and said, 'I myself don't take anything for the service I provide. But of course, I will accept an offering in the name of the Buddha.' When I asked what amount that offering should be, the fortune teller's eyes strayed towards his abacus and he said quickly, 'Fifty dollars should be fine.'

Mak gasped at the price, but the fortune teller assured us that this was a bargain for accessing the knowledge of the universe. And when he put it like that, it seemed churlish to argue. Still, it was a pretty good return for twenty minutes' work, by anybody's calculation.

When we emerged from behind the curtain, the 'free' tuk tuk had, of course, disappeared, and we were left searching for some kind of transport. As we stood on the hot street a small girl walked by in dirty, sweaty clothes, selling jasmine garlands. The smaller garlands were hung all the way up her arms to her shoulders while she held forth three longer ones. I stopped her to buy the longer garlands, all three, because they were so exquisite and I felt so sorry for this little child working through the heat. She named a reasonable price and I paid without bargaining. She handed the flowers to me silently, her big eyes staring at me. 'Has he had his fortune read?' she asked Mak in Khmer.

'Yes, child. How did you know?' he responded.

'I know this is where the Chinese fortune teller is. Was it good or bad?'

'Neither,' responded Mak, 'not good or bad—just normal. I'm not sure I believe any of it.'

The little girl stared at us for a while. 'You'd better believe it,' she said, and then she spoke to me in Khmer, smiled and laughed and ran away.

'What did she say?' I asked, watching as she ran down the crowded street and ducked up into the market.

'She wished you good luck,' said Mak, looking his most serious. 'She has no luck at all, poor little thing, but she wished it for you.'

THE WAY HOME

I was headed home, and took advantage of the necessary stopover in Bangkok to do some shopping and catch up with friends. In Bangkok I bought Angry Birds and Hello Kitty T-shirts for my nephew and niece. While I was bargaining the stallholder was playing Madonna's version of 'Love Don't Live Here Anymore' and I was instantly transported back to my youth and infected with an acutely painful nostalgia. Oh to be young again and feel, really feel, the hurt in that song, instead of merely remembering the hurt refracted back through decades of complacency, comfort and forgetting.

I took the cheap commuter boats all the way to the end of the line, up and down the polluted but still cool Chao Phya River, not caring at all when drops of water splashed my face, though the locals shrieked in horror whenever it happened and held things before them in protection. When I had been here with Panit he was fascinated by the river, and told me that the water was immeasurably deep and filled with a whole world of supernatural beings. 'You have to be Khmer to know about this,' he had said.

After months in Cambodia, and a great deal of time spent in solitude, I found I had cultivated a type of silence that had never really been mine before. This was copied, in part, from my Khmer friends, who would simply be quiet when asked questions they didn't want to answer, and who could easily spend two or even three hours in my company quietly absorbed in their own work, not feeling any kind of need to talk to me. Now I was in Thailand I was struck by the noise and chatter, by how people would talk to me and look at me and ask me interested questions. I was accustomed to being almost invisible in Phnom Penh.

As I get older I occasionally catch sight of myself in the mirror, or hear myself talking, or become aware of the way I relate to people, and I remind myself of my grandmother, or of my spinster Aunt Audrey, two women who couldn't have been more out of place in the exotic locales I so regularly transplant myself to. I am equipped by heritage with a small-town niceness, a plump pleasantness that in fact serves me well as an independent traveller. If I was more slender, more handsome, I would be more dangerous, perhaps. As it is, my homeliness equips me to deal with the world in a uniquely efficient way.

The Cambodians are so resolutely inwardly focused, so rigid in the maintenance of a set of values, that being in Thailand made me nervous. In Bangkok I felt exposed, needed; suddenly people were interested in me again. For these past months in Cambodia I had learned to mask any extreme feelings, to return to myself for answers, comfort and solace instead of seeking explanations outside.

No matter what, I couldn't force myself to wake up early enough in the morning in Bangkok to see the monks on their morning rounds. But in my head I carried that daily image of the grandmothers of Phnom Penh coming to the front of their houses, slipping off their flip-flops and kneeling before the holy men to be blessed. I had always felt blessed too, as though the mumbled, hurried chants somehow crossed the street and enveloped me in their power. I had been slowly cultivating a practice of blessing what is—not what should be, or what I wanted to be. The frustrations of Cambodia and the often perplexing attitudes of its people had been great teachers.

I had been infected, too, with the casual wonder of Cambodian thinking, the willingness to accord the landscape with magical qualities. Mountains were the hallowed remains of sacred crocodiles, and every temple the home of some improbable sacred object which no-one ever saw but all believed in. I wondered how it would feel to return home, where everything was explained and myth and story had no role to play in the commonplace. I had been accustomed to the casual references to shapeshifting and magic and the easy inter-course between ghosts, spirits and humans.

It was also a place where tragic near-history was ever palpable, and everybody lived in the shadow and memory of monstrous acts of mass murder and large-scale destruction. I don't think it is a cliché to say that Cambodia remains a damaged society still coming to terms with the darkness at its heart. This desire to see Cambodia as a bearer of all the tragic impulses of human culture is justly aggravating, particularly to those foreigners who have chosen to live in the new Cambodia and make it their home. But there is no point in denying that the Cambodians themselves use the tragedies of the Pol Pot period as a touchstone for their society's development, and, less helpfully, as an excuse for whatever social ills and injustices that continue. It is also a meme that is very actively propagated by the government and fed to tourists quite intensely. Cambodia grapples with two pasts—the ancient glories of Angkor and the more recent horrors of the Khmer Rouge. The Cambodian people are still balancing the memories of the two, and it is only to be expected that they are both employed, on occasion, cynically. Who would do differently?

In the heavily air-conditioned antiques galleries on Bangkok's riverside developments I came face to face with exquisite Angkorian objects for sale. Who knows when they had left Cambodia, and who knows who stole them and sold them? The beauty of the sculpture is such that it has enchanted the world for over a century now, and seeing it *in situ*, or close enough to it, is creating a whole new tourist phenomenon. Angkor Wat is now so crowded that its own beauty and uniqueness invites its destruction, as perhaps it always did.

I had been obsessed with Cambodia for years, for most of my adult life, and have watched it grow and develop. After months living there I felt keenly its enormous frustrations, but felt enveloped, too, by the very special sentiment of the Khmer, a race of people convinced of their own uniqueness and superiority. To leave Cambodia was to leave a cocoon of wonder and constant aggravation.

In a crass restaurant catering to tourists on Silom Road, I was chatting to a late-middle-aged waiter who was flirting with me outrageously. 'Where do you come from, sir?' he asked.

'Well,' I responded, 'I have been in Cambodia for a few months, but I am headed back home to Australia.'

'Wait!' he cried, rushing back to the kitchen to emerge, moments later, with a shy and handsome youth who smiled at me with strong, white teeth. 'This boy comes from Cambodia! He is our favourite staff member.' Given the camp atmosphere, I could see why. I employed some of my shoddy Khmer, and the young man responded politely but quickly and mercifully switched the conversation back to English.

'Why were you in my country for so long?' he asked, genuinely interested.

'Well, I plan to write a book about it,' I responded.

'Wonderful! What a good man you are to write about my country. I hope you will tell people how beautiful it is, how sweet the Khmer people are, about Angkor Wat, Buddhism, the forests and the king. So much to write about.'

'Yes, so much,' I said, closing the notebook I had been writing in. 'But don't worry, I will do my best.'

BIBLIOGRAPHY

Affonco, Denise 2007, *To the End of Hell*, Reportage Press, London

Amat, Frédéric 2011, *Expatriates' Strange Lives in Cambodia*, Tuk Tuk Editions, Phnom Penh

Asma, Stephen T. 2005, *The Gods Drink Whiskey: Stumbling toward enlightenment in the land of the tattered Buddha*, Harper San Francisco, San Francisco

Baumgärtel, Tilman (ed) 2011, *Dontrey: The Music of Cambodia*, Department of Media and Communication, Royal University of Phnom Penh, Phnom Penh

Becker, Elizabeth 2010, *Bophana: Love in the time of the Khmer Rouge*, Cambodia Daily Press, Phnom Penh

Brinkley, Joel 2011, *Cambodia's Curse*, Black Ink, Collingwood

Castagna, Felicity 2011, *Small Indiscretions: Stories of travel in Asia*, Transit Lounge Publishing, Yarraville

Chanda, Nayan 1986, *Brother Enemy: The war after the war*, Collier Books, New York

Chandler, David 2008, *A History of Cambodia*, 4th edition, Silkworm Books, Chiang Mai

Harris, Ian 2006, *Cambodian Buddhism: History and Practice*, Silkworm Books, Chiang Mai

Imam, Vannary 2000, *When Elephants Fight: A memoir*, Allen & Unwin, St Leonards

Jacobsen, Trudy 2006, '*Maha Upasika*, women's morality, and merit in Middle Cambodia', *Siksacakr: The Journal of Cambodia Research. Special issue on Buddhism*, no. 8–9 (2006–2007), pp. 13–19

James, Kate 2012, *When Gods Collide: An unbeliever's pilgrimage along India's Coramandel Coast*, Hardie Grant Books, Richmond

Jones, Marie D. and Flaxman, Larry 2009, *11:11: The Time Prompt Phenomenon*, New Page Books, Franklin Lakes

Khun, Vichea and He, Chenthy 2011, *Habit: A New Practical Concept to Success*, AEU, Phnom Penh

Kornfield, Jack and Siegel, Dr Daniel 2011, *Bringing Home the Dharma: Awakening right where you are*, Shambhala, Boston

McDaniel, Justin Thomas 2011, *The Lovelorn Ghost and the Magical Monk: Practicing Buddhism in modern Thailand*, Columbia University Press, New York

McGavin, Nicky 2012, 'Discover Battambang', *Cambodia AsiaLIFE*, issue 65 (May), pp. 44–45

Nath, Vann 1998, *A Cambodian Prison Portrait: One Year in the Khmer Rouge's S-21*, White Lotus, Bangkok

Osborne, Milton 1994, *Sihanouk: Prince of Darkness, Prince of Light*, Allen & Unwin, St Leonards

Otis, Daniel 2012, 'Fighting for the family', *South-East Asia Globe*, February issue, pp. 76–81

Ponnareth, Penn 2008, *Rainbow Sky Surface*, Buddhist Institute Printing House, Phnom Penh

Roveda, Vittorio and Yem, Sothorn 2009, *Buddhist Painting in Cambodia*, River Books, Bangkok

Saunders, Doug 2010, *Arrival City: The final migration and our next world*, Pantheon Books, New York

Sitwell, Sacheverell 1962 *The Red Chapels of Banteai Srei*, Weidenfeld & Nicolson, London

Snook, Laura J. 2012, 'Courting the Kim Clan', *South-East Asia Globe*, February issue, pp. 34–35

Taylor, Philip 2007, 'Modernity and re-enchantment in post-revolutionary Vietnam' in *Modernity and Re-enchantment*, ISEAS Publishing, Singapore, pp. 1–56

Vachon, Michelle 2012, 'Professor Chandler's Cambodia', *The Cambodia Daily Weekend*, issue 737, May 5–6, pp. 4–7

Vajiramedhi, V. 2010, *Happiness is Here and Now*, Amarin Publishing, Bangkok

Vannak, Huy 2010, *Bou Meng: A Survivor from Khmer Rouge Prison S-21,* Documentation Center of Cambodia, Phnom Penh